THE PROBLEM WITH BANKS

About the Authors

Lena Rethel is Assistant Professor of International Political Economy at the University of Warwick. Her research focuses on capital market development, the emergence and challenges of Islamic finance and the relationship of finance, debt and development. She has co-edited two collections on the political economy of the subprime crisis and a journal special issue on global governance in crisis.

Timothy J. Sinclair is Associate Professor of International Political Economy at the University of Warwick. In 2001/02 he was a visiting scholar at Harvard University. His research is concerned with the politics of global finance and theories of global governance. The paperback edition of his book *The New Masters of Capital: American Bond Rating Agencies and the Politics of Creditworthiness* was published in 2008.

THE PROBLEM WITH BANKS

LENA RETHEL & TIMOTHY J. SINCLAIR

Zed Books

LONDON | NEW YORK

The Problem with Banks was first published in 2012 by
Zed Books Ltd, 7 Cynthia Street, London N1 9JF, UK
and Room 400, 175 Fifth Avenue, New York, NY 10010, USA

www.zedbooks.co.uk

Designed and typeset in Monotype Bulmer
by illuminati, Grosmont
Index by John Barker
Cover designed by www.alice-marwick.co.uk
Printed and bound by CPI Group (UK) Ltd,
Croydon CRO 4YY

Distributed in the USA exclusively by Palgrave Macmillan, a division of
St Martin's Press, LLC, 175 Fifth Avenue, New York, NY 10010, USA

A catalogue record for this book is available from the British Library
Library of Congress Cataloging in Publication Data available

ISBN 978 1 84813 939 8 hb
ISBN 978 1 84813 938 1 pb

CONTENTS

To our students, and to those who work to make
our world – including the banks – better

GLOSSARY

ABS	Asset-backed securities, e.g. bond based on mortgage payments
bank run	Mass withdrawal of deposits, fearing bank insolvency
Banking Act 1933	Also known as the Glass–Steagall Act 1933; Depression-era US legislation which separated commercial and investment banking until repealed
Basel Accords	Banking supervision agreements, including capital reserves, agreed in Basel, Switzerland
BCBS	Basel Committee on Banking Supervision
BCCI	Bank of Credit and Commerce International
BIS	Bank for International Settlements
Bretton Woods system	Post-World War II international monetary system established in 1944 at a conference in Bretton Woods, New Hampshire
CDO	Collateralized debt obligation; a type of ABS
Chinese walls	Internal barrier intended to avoid conflicts of interest
commercial bank	Banks mainly in the business of taking deposits from and lending to business
constitutive rules	Social practices which bring something into being, such as chess or the financial system
countercyclical	Actions or institutions which dampen prevailing economic and financial trends

CRA	Credit rating agency, such as Moody's Investors Service
diachronic view	A view of the workings of social life which incorporates the immanent potential for change in all institutions and processes
disintermediation	Elimination of middlemen such as wholesalers, as customer and provider deal with each other directly
Dodd–Frank Act 2010	US legislative response to the global financial crisis that started in 2007
doxa	Prevailing mental framework or way of thinking
EMH	Efficient Markets Hypothesis
ERM	Exchange Rate Mechanism
Fed	US Federal Reserve System
financial disintermediation	Cutting out the middleman, such as banks, in financial markets
financial engineering	Mathematically informed efforts to maximize returns through innovation
G20	Group of Twenty finance ministers and central bank governors
Glass–Steagall Act 1933	Also known as the Banking Act 1933; Depression-era US legislation which separated commercial and investment banking until repealed
Gramm–Leach–Bliley Act 1999	Also known as the Financial Modernization Act 1999; US legislation which repealed Glass–Steagall Act 1933/Banking Act 1933
Great Panic/ Great Freeze	Unwillingness of most banks in rich countries to transact with each other in 2007–09
Group of Thirty	Group of leading business and academic figures who discuss key economic and financial policy issues
ICB	Independent Commission on Banking
IMF	International Monetary Fund
investment bank	Bank which raises funds for clients in capital markets, and trades there on own account, such as Goldman Sachs before the global financial crisis
lender of last resort	Bailing out of systemically important institutions, usually by central bank

MPP	Macroprudential policymaking
ordoliberal	Liberalism which sees key role for state in setting rules of the game
PRA	Prudential Regulatory Authority: part of the Bank of England; set to replace the UK Financial Services Authority as prudential regulator
procyclical	Actions or institutions which amplify current economic and financial trends
proprietary trading	Trading on the bank's own account, rather than on behalf of the bank's clients
prudential regulation	Regulation of the actions of financial institutions
regulative rules	Rules which govern an already existing activity, such as driving
regulatory arbitrage	The effort to get around regulative rules
Sarbanes–Oxley Act 2002	US legislation passed in the wake of the Enron scandal of 2001
savings and loan crisis	Failure of US savings banks in the late 1980s and early 1990s after deregulation
securitization	Transformation of illiquid bank loans into tradable securities
self-regulation	Regulation relying on market institutions themselves, assuming they know more about the industry than does government
shadow banking system	Transactions outside the core regulated financial system, by institutions such as hedge funds, structured investment vehicles
structural regulation	Rules about how an industry such as banking and finance is organized
synchronic view	Internal logic of a system
SIFIs	Systemically important financial institutions
tabloid beauty contest metaphor	Keynes's illustration of the self-referential nature of financial markets
too big to fail	Another way to refer to SIFIs
Triple A	Highest grade credit rating: AAA or Aaa

universal bank	A bank which incorporates commercial, investment and retail activities, such as Bank of America, HSBC and Deutsche Bank
VAR	Value-at-risk, a way of establishing the total risk exposure of a balance sheet
Volcker rule	Part of the Dodd–Frank Act, this bans proprietary trading by US deposit-taking banks from July 2012
yield	Rate of return of a financial instrument such as a bond

PREFACE

The Occupy Wall Street demonstrations which began in New York in September 2011 using the slogan 'We are the 99%' kicked off a wider US and global protest movement against corporate greed and the dominance of financial services in business and politics. By early November 2011 protests inspired by the New York movement had occurred in around 900 cities worldwide. Although we offer this book as a thoughtful contribution to the debate about banks, we understand the frustrations the global financial system and corporate capitalism generate. We think a better world is possible, and we hope this book can make a contribution to building that world.

We argue in this book that banks are very troublesome institutions. They borrow short in the form of demand deposits and lend long. Their profitable lending opportunities are being taken away from them by the capital markets, forcing them to innovate and engage in sophisticated financial engineering. We suggest that there is a lack of appreciation of how government shapes the motivations of banks, and how banks evolve as institutions alongside states. Unlike most other books about banks, which assume banks are given or natural, we argue that government has a major role in creating and shaping bank behaviour. Government does not just regulate banks, but actually creates or constitutes what banks are and what banks do. However, few who make public policy recognize this deeper, constitutive role of government in making banks.

Increasingly, banks are focused on the short-term or synchronic outlook, and neglect diachronic issues such as investment in the productive assets that will create prosperity and jobs in the future. Banks have ceased to be strategic institutions that make key decisions about how our society will evolve, even as they retain a systemic position in our global economy. If banks do not act in the public interest when they are so important to public welfare, and have to be bailed out when they fail, the case for their reform is more vital than ever. Our argument is developed as follows.

Chapter 1 considers how banking crises have led to more regulation, and how this has systematically influenced the evolution of banks. It pays particular attention to the key argument we propose, namely that governments have played a pivotal role in shaping how banks have evolved over the centuries and that this has to be taken into account when it comes to creating space for any meaningful discussion of banking reform.

What exactly are banks? Chapter 2 takes a closer look at the nature of banks. Banks lend long term and borrow short term. This makes them vulnerable to any loss of confidence in their ability to cover demands on their funds. This perennial issue is at the heart of most crises, including the latest. However, in recent years, the so-called maturity mismatch of bank lending has been exacerbated by the fact that banks also lent more than they borrowed from depositors. In so doing, they put extra pressure on the system. This chapter suggests that we have to think of banks as players in a metaphorical confidence game. However, ultimately confidence in banks does not derive so much from their proficiency in the game as opposed to their successful moves to free-ride on the efforts of other players, namely states. In so doing, the participation of states in the game alters the rules of the game itself. Bank free-riding is not solely restricted to bailouts, which have figured so prominently in recent media discourse, but includes issues such as the role of states as enforcers of the rules of the game (e.g. property and creditor rights as well as financial regulation broadly conceived) and as controllers of who is allowed to play the game (e.g. market access and concentration). The chapter identifies two drivers for the recent transformation of banks from market authorities to market players: progressive financial disintermediation and increased reliance on self-regulation.

The two subsequent chapters scrutinize the evolution and transformation of banks in recent decades. They suggest that banks have undergone a shift from market authorities to market players. Chapter 3 looks at the impact of financial disintermediation on banking. Banks have increasingly had to compete as lenders with more efficient and lower cost capital markets. This competition has transformed banks from market authorities to participants, and motivated them to search for yield through financial innovation such as asset-backed securities. To protect interest income in a world where corporations tend to raise funds in capital markets, banks increasingly targeted loans at households. However, this change in banks' activities was underpinned by the perception of policymakers that diversifying funding sources by creating liquid capital markets was for the public good, as was widening access to credit. As a consequence, states acted as important facilitators of financial disintermediation and the increasingly synchronic market logic focused on profit maximization, rather than on diachronic concerns about growth through the development of productive capacities.

Chapter 4 scrutinizes the interplay between increased self-regulation and the behaviour of banks. Governments changed their approach to banking regulation between the end of the Bretton Woods system in the 1970s and the onset of the global financial crisis in 2007. Regulatory authorities lost confidence in their ability to regulate banks. Instead, they sought to push responsibility for prudent behaviour onto the institutions themselves. Underlying this shift towards self-regulation was the notion that banks are simply too complex, acting in a rapidly evolving environment, for regulators to keep up. This changed not only the way that banks conducted their operations, but the nature of banks themselves. A result of the drive towards self-regulation was that banks tended to get bigger. This was based on the notion that size reflects success in business and as a logical consequence bigger banks are more sophisticated and thus better able to regulate themselves, never mind economies of scale and scope. Little attention was paid to the idea that it was actually regulatory arbitrage, and not necessarily business acumen, which drove the growth of the big banks in the run-up to the global financial crisis. Again, this chapter supports the notion that public policy has been fundamental in shaping banks. Moreover, it did so in a constitutive sense as opposed to in a merely reactionary regulative manner.

In Chapter 5 we assess a range of proposals that have been made to reform banking regulation and say why we think these reforms will not solve the problem with banks. More specifically, we will look at three issue areas in more detail: macroprudential policies (including some of the new Basel III specifications), a ban on proprietary trading (the so-called Volcker rule) and proposals about breaking up the banks to achieve a more competitive market structure. We argue that all these proposals ignore the constitutive role played by government when it comes to shaping the nature of banks, and the need for a diachronic approach to understanding these institutions. Thus, in our opinion just implementing the Volcker rule, breaking up the banks, or creating the mechanisms for improved macroprudential regulation are not sufficient to rid us of the problem with banks. Indeed, it is questionable whether the problem with banks can ever be fully solved, and if this is the case, then a more fundamental rethinking of public policy and its relation to banks is necessary.

This is not to say that we should despair. In concluding we explore alternative ways of regulating and shaping banks. Thus, the Conclusion sets out our own reform agenda, suggesting that a more incisive view of change is needed, which relates to the very purpose of banking institutions. First of all, a broad societal consensus is required. Also, when it comes to the more intricate details of reform proposals, more creative solutions are necessary. This could mean, for example, entrusting separate organizations with the safekeeping of deposits and the generation of funds for investment, whose risk is more clearly spelled out. This implies that depositors in the future would either have to be satisfied with no return on their savings or accept the very real possibility of investment losses. The question is, is it the function of banks to generate public and individual wealth themselves (with a similar potential to destroy it), or should banks be no more than market authorities rather than market players?

A number of people helped us develop our thoughts along the way, including the anonymous reviewers of the proposal and the manuscript, a conference audience at the University of Warwick in September 2011 and Ken Barlow, our enthusiastic editor at Zed Books, whose close attention to the manuscript was greatly appreciated.

This volume has been motivated by our shared sense that banks are very troublesome but need not be such problematic institutions if we first recognize that society makes banks what they are. We have dedicated this book to our students and to all those who are still optimistic enough not to be taken in by the frequently heard notion that there is no alternative. History and our lives are about making change.

Lena Rethel and Timothy J. Sinclair
Coventry

ONE

BANKS IN CRISIS
TIME AND TIME AGAIN

Banks of all sorts are troubled institutions. The cost of public bailouts associated with the subprime crisis in the United States alone may be as high as US$5 trillion. What is the problem with banks? Why do they seem to be at the centre of economic and financial turmoil down through the ages? And was there anything different about the most recent banking crisis? These are the central questions this book seeks to answer. Although there is of course an established literature on banking, this largely focuses on the financial operations of banks considered in abstract process terms. Banks are conceptualized as institutions that have emerged to fulfil certain functions in society (e.g. to safeguard deposits and to intermediate between savers and borrowers). Thus, their operations are thought to follow a rather timeless functionalist logic. This volume, however, considers banks in terms of the specific historical circumstances they face, and how these circumstances have changed the identity of banks from market authorities to market participants, transforming their behaviour and appetite for risk. We think there is a lack of appreciation of how government shapes what banks do, and how they evolve as institutions. Again, most of the expert literature merely sees government as a constraint on banks. We argue that what governments do in terms of regulation shapes banks and their very motivations. In order to understand banks one must understand their link with states and how this has changed over time.

Importantly, given the recent global financial crisis, we intend to discuss new and alternative ways of regulating and shaping banks that go beyond simply putting into place new rules of conduct that banks will do their utmost to avoid. However, before we do so in the subsequent chapters of this book, let us first consider the crisis-prone nature of banks over time and across regions and jurisdictions and the public responses that it has drawn. The following discussion looks at both how banking crises have led to more regulation, but also at how this in turn has systematically influenced the evolution of banks. It pays particular attention to the key argument that we propose, namely that governments have played a pivotal role in shaping how banks have evolved over the centuries and that this has to be taken into account when it comes to creating space for any meaningful discussion of banking reform.

Regulating Banks

In 2008, at the height of the global credit crunch, pundits warned that the world was about to see 'the mother of all bank runs' (Roubini 2008). However, the capitalist world has been marred by bank runs and banking crises for centuries. Indeed, it is perhaps one of the more positive effects of this – and previous – financial crises that they have spurred a wave of literature that attempts to put financial crises in historical perspective (see e.g. Reinhart and Rogoff 2009; Kindleberger 2000). What we can learn from this literature is that – more often than not – banks have been at the centre of financial crises. Banks have been both deeply implicated in their emergence and also strongly vulnerable to their occurrence.

This fate has been shared by developed and developing countries alike. As Reinhart and Rogoff (2009: 141) put it,

> Although many now-advanced economies have graduated from a history of serial default on sovereign debt or very high inflation, so far graduation from banking crises has proven elusive ... banking crises have long impacted rich and poor countries alike.

If there is a difference between countries, it seems that international financial centres are more prone to banking crises. Indeed, if we look at the experience of the last 100 years, the USA with its deep and sophisticated financial system has suffered more heavily from financial crises than any other country. Economic development on its own certainly is not sufficient as a cure against banking crises.

What is the problem with banks? Why is their history marred with crises and yet why have they – despite their seemingly troublesome nature – come to play such an important role in everyday economic and political life? To answer this question, it is important to take a closer look at the historical evolution of banks and their relationship with states. Indeed, the enduring existence of banks would have been impossible without the constitutive role played by states and government regulation. Over the centuries, crises have played a pivotal role in this development (Grossman 2010; Banner 1998).

Banks are not an invention of the capitalist era. The existence of institutions fulfilling a safekeeping function, one of the major tasks of banks, dates back several millennia. Indeed, in the ancient world, temples in Egypt and Mesopotamia were solidly constructed and often considered refuges, so served the safekeeping function (Hoggson 1926). However, modern forms of banking are usually traced back to developments in the city states of late medieval/early Renaissance Italy such as Genoa and Florence (Hildreth 2001). There exists a close relationship between the emergence of states as modern forms of political community and the lending activities of bankers (Tilly 1992; Kindleberger 1993). Thus, the very political nature of banks from their origins should not be underestimated. Banks, such as that owned by the Rothschilds, extended loans to finance the military activities of kings, including England's campaigns in the Napoleonic wars. Nevertheless, with the growing importance of fractional reserve banking, where only a relatively small proportion of a bank's demand deposits are actually held as readily available reserves, the frequency of banking crises increased dramatically. And so did the complexity of state–bank interaction as states increasingly strove to regulate the conduct of banks. In the following discussion, we first look at motivations to regulate banks more generally, before turning to more recent efforts to coordinate the regulation of banks on an international level and how this again has contributed to changes in the nature and quality of banking regulation and operations.

Ad hoc efforts to support bank-like financial institutions vis-à-vis financial instability can be traced back over millennia. Thus, in Davis's (1910) humorous account of the business panic of 33 AD, where lenders were threatened by a loss of confidence caused by a series of alleged and real business failures, the spread of financial instability, complete with a series of runs on lending institutions, was only halted when the Emperor Tiberius stepped in as lender of last resort. Historically in Europe, the emergence of modern banking practice was strongly linked to a series of banking and financial crises such as the South Sea and Mississippi crises of early-eighteenth-century Britain and France. In striking similarity to the recent global financial crisis, both crises revolved around a bank-driven monetary expansion, generated by Sword Blade bank in England and John Law's bank in France. Other companies sprang up to take advantage of the speculative fever, including one formed 'for carrying on an undertaking of great advantage, but nobody to know what it is' (Galbraith 1993: 49; Kindleberger and Aliber 2005: 165). The nineteenth century, often praised as an era of relative international monetary stability, bore witness to a range of banking and financial crises, but also laid the foundations for more elaborate approaches towards the public regulation of banks.

Initially there was little difference or even separation between the private and the public spheres in banking (Grossman 2010; Kindleberger 1993). More specifically, central banking as a distinct regulatory practice only arrived relatively late in the history of banks, as the chequered history of the Bank of England, incorporated in 1694 by royal charter as a private company, illustrates. While the state had to develop the tools necessary to regulate banks and to intervene in financial markets, the onset of the industrial age brought massive growth in the banking industry. This was accompanied by increasingly frequent banking crises that at the time mainly hit the more developed countries that had more advanced banking systems (see also Figure 2.1). Indeed, Reinhart and Rogoff (2008: 13) suggest that in particular France, the United Kingdom and the United States stand out in this respect, having been hit by a banking crisis 15, 12 and 13 times respectively since 1800.

Like Europe, the United States has not been spared banking crises. Indeed, in 1792, shortly after gaining independence, the nascent nation was hit by a financial crisis caused by speculation in the stock of the Bank of New York, with rival parties trying to cause the stock to rise and fall, precipitating a bank run. Treasury Secretary Alexander Hamilton stemmed the crisis by intervening in the banking system (Sylla et al. 2009). A more dramatic wave of financial panic and bank failures swept the United States in 1818–19. Ever since then, the USA has suffered from periodic outbreaks of more and less severe banking crises and bank failures, with the panic of 1907, the financial crisis during the Great Depression of the 1930s, the savings and loan crisis of the late 1980s and early 1990s, and the subprime crisis of the late 2000s being the most dramatic.

The 1907 financial panic came about after the failure of a trust company at the centre of Wall Street speculation (Bruner and Carr 2007). Calamity was avoided by cooperation between major banks, led by J.P. Morgan, the world's best-known and most powerful banker. Again, the American government initially relied largely on ad hoc mechanisms, before moving towards a more systematic response to banking crises. Thus, a massive effort to (better) regulate banks was undertaken as a response to the 1930s' crisis when the American banking system suffered heavily during the economic turmoil of the interwar period. All in all, about 9,000 banks, a third of all banks in the United States, had to be closed during the period from 1929 to 1933 (Galbraith 1977: 202). As is well known, the American government reacted by introducing a range of far-reaching banking reforms.

The 1933 Banking Act (also known as the Glass–Steagall Act) compelled the splitting up of banks according to the type of business they were undertaking (commercial or investment banking). It also introduced a system of deposit insurance and limits on the interest that could be charged by banks. However, it has to be noted that this segmentation of the banking market was built on trajectories within the American regulatory system that can be traced back at least to the Civil War (White 1982).

In the post-World War II period, the segmented banking system increasingly came under challenge as the economic centre of gravity moved to the USA. The regulatory efforts of the 1930s failed to make the US financial system crisis-proof. A series of bank failures in the 1970s and the resurgence of free-market ideas triggered a spate of deregulatory efforts that increasingly undermined the provisions of the 1933 Banking Act. Along these lines, from the 1990s onwards, there was a decisive move away from the segmented market model and towards a more European-style universal banking model in the United States as commercial banks (deposit-taking institutions with retail and wholesale operations) sought to operate in the capital markets. This was compounded by the eventual repeal of the 1933 Banking Act in favour of the Financial Modernization Act (also known as the Gramm–Leach–Bliley Act) in 1999 (Crockett et al. 2003). Recent efforts to reregulate the American banking system in the wake of the subprime financial crisis have to be seen against this backdrop.

East Asia, although less visible in mainstream discourses on banking crises and regulation, also suffered its fair share of banking instability and crises, even prior to concerns about the effectiveness of local banks during the Asian financial crisis of 1997–98 (see e.g. Hill 2003 and other contributions in this special issue). During the colonial period, Western merchant banks brought modern banking practices to the region (Ji 2003; Cheng 2003). Their claims to extraterritoriality put them outside the control of local authorities. Indirectly this already foreshadowed some of the problems with the supervision and regulation of transnational banking groups. In recent times, the most dramatic such occurrence was the collapse of Barings following wild speculation by one of its Singapore-based employees in the mid-1990s. The incident exposed gaps in the international supervisory framework and problems with the coordination of home country (UK)/host country (Singapore) supervision (Herring 2005).

Long before then, and exacerbated by the arrival of modern banks and banking operations, local financial institutions also exhibited vulnerabilities and repeatedly succumbed to crisis. China suffered from financial instability and banking crises in the late nineteenth and early twentieth centuries, such as the Shanghai rubber stock-market crisis of 1910, where speculation in rubber stocks turned awry, resulting in the closure of domestic banks (Ji 2003: 93). Japan's 1927 banking crisis affected its colonial dependency, Taiwan. State-building and the promotion of modern practices of banking were closely linked in the region. This is well illustrated by the diverse crisis experiences in the banking systems of Southeast Asia (Cook 2008; Hamilton-Hart 2002; Singh 1984: 271).

Banking troubles again lay at the heart of Japan's lost decade of the 1990s and also spread from Japan to the wider East Asia region in the 1997–98 financial crisis (Amyx 2004; King 2001). The Asian financial crisis demonstrated how interlinked national financial sectors had become and how bank instabilities in one country could rapidly spill over into other jurisdictions. It also exposed the vulnerabilities that were created when highly politicized banking sectors met with the vagaries of disintermediated international portfolio investment flows (Haggard 2000). As a consequence of the crisis and the challenges that it was seen to have posed to 'business as usual', Asian policymakers felt increasingly compelled to implement financial sector reforms and, at least to some extent, to adopt international best practices (Walter 2008).

While this account of the history of banks and their evolution in Europe, the United States and East Asia is by necessity broad-brushed, it nevertheless highlights the fact that banks around the globe are very crisis-prone institutions. This has served as a major justification for states to devise rules for the conduct of banks.

The emergence of modern states and modern banking systems has been closely intertwined. Whereas for a long time banks had had to deal with defaulting sovereigns, now states came increasingly to incur the costs of defaulting banks. States had to develop the tools to move from ad hoc interventionism to more formal mechanisms of bank regulation. Yet, in the process, responses to banking crises also fundamentally shaped the boundaries for future financial arrangements. In so doing, they did not just constrain but indeed created the behaviour of banks, thus setting in train pathologies for future crises.

Mainstream accounts of banking regulation identify a range of reasons for governments to regulate banks. According to Kroszner (1998), these can be divided into two broad categories: those that focus on the orderly provision of banking services, in particular to prevent conflicts of interest and establish the fairness of trans-actions, and those related to financial stability considerations. Explanations falling in the first category draw attention to the important role that banks play as economic actors and their traditional functions such as mobilizing savings, intermediating between borrowers and savers, and monitoring and disciplining borrowers on behalf of savers. Yet banks as profit-maximizing organizations are more than neutral go-betweens (Palazzo and Rethel 2008: 195). Thus, banks are prone to conflicts of interest that are deemed to distract or prevent them from fulfilling their economic role in an efficient manner (Kroszner 1998; Crockett et al. 2003). According to this view, governments (have to) step in as regulators to correct market imperfections.

We suggest that the conventional view that focuses on banks as economic actors, operating in a somewhat distinct economic sphere, pays too little attention to their role as social and political actors and thus underplays their systemic significance. It offers only an incomplete portrait of what they do. Thus, banks and their regulation should not be conceived in largely abstract process terms but linked to wider political and social developments. An important such development over the last century has been the expansion of the democratic franchise. However, when it comes to bank regulation, democratic expansion puts pressure on governments to protect the savings of voters, as well as their tax payments (Rosas 2009; Thirkell-White 2009). In this regard, an important driver of regulation/public policy highlighted by the discourses surrounding the recent global financial crisis is to avoid the costs of future bailouts, given the perceived necessity for governments to step in as lenders of last resort to prevent systemic financial crises. Reinhart and Rogoff (2009: 142) suggest that focusing on the costs of bailouts associated with banking crises presents us with only part of the picture. The implications for tax revenue and public debt are far more significant. According to their calculations, modern banking crises have resulted in an average increase of real government debt by 86 per cent during the three years following the crisis. This order of magnitude applies equally for developed and developing countries.

This leads us to the second category of explanation: bank regulation as a response to their inherent (in)stability. Banks borrow short term from their depositors and (as has become increasingly important in recent years) the money market, and lend long term. This gives rise to an intrinsic contradiction as banks sit at the nexus of two competing temporal logics. It is the core of a bank's business to manage this intrinsic contradiction. Here, as we discuss in more detail in the next chapter, bank regulation also serves as an important confidence-building measure. If there is something that sets the recent crisis apart from previous crises, it is that, at least for a short moment, it put into question the confidence placed in the constitutive rules that underpin contemporary financial and regulatory practice (Sinclair 2009).

Well-regulated banks are held to be a public good by both
market liberals and interventionists, although with varying
conclusions with regard to policy implications. However, in
recent years there has been a third (crisis-driven) motivation for
regulating banks, and that relates to access to credit. Not only
financial stability but now also access to credit has increasingly
come to be perceived as a public good (Rethel 2010a; Seabrooke
2010). Whilst for centuries the power to borrow had largely been
a sovereign prerogative, and to a lesser extent that of a small
elite, it has turned into a mass phenomenon, although there still
remain stark differences in the availability and cost of credit.
Indeed, over the last few decades making credit more broadly
available has emerged as a key policy priority. This has to be seen
against the backdrop of stagnation in real wage growth in much
of North America and Europe, and the importance of economic
performance for regime legitimacy in a wide range of East Asian
economies. In this process, banks have had a key role. Thus, what
we have witnessed in recent years was perhaps not 'just' a crisis
in finance and regulation, but more generally a crisis of a system
of financial capitalism of which the recent global financial crisis
was just a symptom (Crouch 2009; Gamble 2009).

The domestic regulation of banks has a rich history. Efforts to
coordinate bank regulation internationally are of a much shorter
provenance. Despite finance often being seen as one of the most
globalized sectors of the international economy, local financial
regulation continues to exhibit stark variations and is organized very differently in different parts of the world, a fact to
which the comparative political economy literature bears testimony (Rosenbluth and Schaap 2003; Vogel 1996; Zysman 1983).
Indeed, national bank regulation varies along several dimensions,
including the organizational structure of regulatory authority,
legal and fiscal frameworks, and the capacity to enforce bank

regulation. As a result of this variety, banks work differently in different countries and susceptibility to financial crisis varies (see e.g. Busch 2009).

While we acknowledge this variation, we nevertheless suggest there has been a more profound convergence in recent years with regard to the principles underpinning banking regulation, simultaneously reinforced by and reinforcing the way financial markets, most importantly banks, operate. These changes have been shaped by a number of global–domestic interactions. They include the emergence and proliferation of transnational banking groups, increased efforts to coordinate bank regulation internationally, and a decisive shift towards regulating banks via prudential rules on both domestic and global levels. We will briefly characterize these changes in the remainder of this section. However, it is worth noting that these transitions have to be understood against the background of wider economic, political and social developments, which will be discussed in more detail in Chapters 3 and 4.

The emergence and growing salience of transnational banking groups has been a major trend that has characterized the last three decades. There is a broad consensus that this requires co-ordination among bank regulators. The two major bank collapses in Britain in the early and mid-1990s, namely those of BCCI and Barings, were remarkable not so much for their lack of systemic consequences, but because they highlighted the difficulties of regulating and supervising internationally active banks. Whilst internationally active banks have existed for centuries, the sheer scale that global banking activity has reached in recent years is unprecedented.

The growing importance of transnational banking groups has exacerbated problems with regulatory arbitrage. Regulatory arbitrage refers to the process in which a bank takes advantage of the possibility of being regulated by a more 'accommodating' regulator (Tirole 2010: 30). Regulatory arbitrage increasingly occurs between jurisdictions. Since the demise of the Bretton Woods system in the 1970s, it has become a problem of global proportions, even more so as the capacity of transnational banking groups to actively exploit differences in national regulation has encouraged regulatory competition between countries, especially between the United States and the United Kingdom. Nonetheless, international regulatory arbitrage is not a simple product of globalization. Instead, it is a socio-political construct, encouraging the behaviour of 'choose your own regulator'. It strongly supports our argument that – inadvertently or not – states shape banks at the level of their very motivations.

The fact that banks conduct business in a growing range of countries and regions and thus are exposed to different regulatory regimes has also turned out to be an important driver of the co-ordination of banking regulation on a global scale. Hence, in the decades since the collapse of the original Bretton Woods system, there have been increased efforts towards the international co-ordination of bank regulation. However, it is important to note that the global coordination of regulation seems to be politically more feasible with regard to certain issue areas such as capital adequacy rules and provisions against money laundering than in others. Thus, for example, the global financial crisis highlighted that there remain strong barriers against improved international coordination in critical areas such as insolvency regulation.

It has become increasingly clear in recent years that regional coordination of bank regulation should also not be ignored. As a matter of fact, banking regulation on the European level is the best and most advanced example of this trend (Mügge 2011). However, tentative steps towards more coordinated regional banking regulation and supervision have also been undertaken in the East Asia

TABLE 1.1   The world's 1,000 biggest banks by region of origin,
1990–2010

	1990	2000	2010
EU		288	278
Rest of Europe	444	100	41
USA	222	199	169
Middle East	58	77	90
Latin America	40	50	44
Japan	112	116	100
Asia	104	150	221
Rest of world	20	20	57

Source: Adapted from Timewell 2010/*The Banker*.

region. Indeed, this is becoming more important as a growing number of the biggest international banking groups are originating outside the US–EU core, mainly in ex-Japan Asia (see Table 1.1). The global financial crisis accelerated this trend (Helleiner and Pagliari 2011: 176). These different levels of regulation can shape each other, especially as usually rules designed on the international level have to be implemented by local authorities (for example, the 1988 Basel Accord and its revisions, discussed in Chapter 4). Nevertheless, the global financial crisis has demonstrated that stark discrepancies remain.

Increased attempts at the international coordination of banking regulation also fed into and exacerbated the convergence of the norms and principles underpinning regulatory efforts. Thus, over the last two decades there was a marked shift towards regulating banks via prudential rules. Again, global–domestic interactions were an important driver of this trend, in particular with regard to the Basel Capital Adequacy Accords. In this regard, Rosenbluth and Schaap (2003) also cite the specificities of financial systems that have one form or another of deposit insurance as a key motivation for globally coordinated prudential regulation. Via prudential regulation, states were trying to deflect the cost of a crisis onto banks themselves – unsuccessfully, as the global financial crisis has shown.

The international coordination of banking regulation was also seen as an important means to limit regulatory competition. Indeed, it can be very costly for governments to go it alone when it comes to bank regulation. This is why government and market actors, especially in key financial centres such as the USA and the UK, have undertaken concerted efforts towards the better international coordination of the regulation of banks, in so doing imposing their understanding of regulatory 'best practice' on an ever-growing range of countries. Indeed, Oatley and Nabors (1998) argue that the main purpose of the 1988 Basel Accord was not so much to address market failure as to redistribute the costs of financial regulation, ostensibly creating a level playing field for internationally active banks. Moreover, the Basel system, especially the updated Basel II version, also became increasingly linked to self-regulation, as is discussed in more detail in Chapter 4.

As banks were becoming bigger through domestic mergers and cross-border mergers, this increased the lobbying power of financial firms. It made certain dimensions of international coordination more difficult. It also increased the time lag between private-sector developments and regulatory responses (Dewatripont and Rochet 2010). Against this background, the shift towards prudential regulation as the predominant regulatory device is somewhat understandable. However, these global and domestic regulatory dynamics did not prevent the outbreak of the global financial crisis of 2007–09. Neither domestic regulation nor international coordination did much to stand in the way of cross-border arbitrage, and banks became increasingly unfettered (Moshirian 2011). By focusing their efforts on the prudential regulation of banking activities, states did not prevent banks from conducting very problematic activities, but actually made possible an ever-growing range of these activities as long as the banks stuck to the regulations about how to do these things. They thus contributed to fostering an increasingly short-termist and profit-driven logic of bank operations. In hindsight, it is very clear that states should not have divested themselves of so much of their regulatory toolkit and should have retained a more holistic notion of the purposes and practices of regulation.

The Argument

The importance of regulation is clearly acknowledged in the mainstream literature. Thus, Kroszner (1998: 48) states that 'regulation rather than competition determines a bank's range of products and services, the types of its assets and liabilities, the legal structure of its organization, the extent of control of non-financial firms by banks and of banks by non-financial firms.' Nevertheless, there is a lack of appreciation of how government shapes the nature of banks themselves and how they evolve as institutions. Government is not merely a constraint on banks. In fact, public policy shapes banks' very motivations. The point is that the existing mainstream literature takes banks as given or natural. It thus tends to underplay the role played by government in creating and shaping bank behaviour. In so doing, the significance of bank regulation goes well beyond just designing and implementing rules of conduct for banks.

It might be opportune to consider the writings of the philosopher John Searle. His approach helps us understand that collectively shared ideas are not ephemeral but material to the problem with banks. His thinking is also useful in helping us distinguish between the surface of things and the core. Searle suggested it is possible to distinguish regulative rules that 'regulate antecedently or independently existing forms of behaviour' from a much more architectural form of rule (Searle 1969: 33). These more structural or constitutive rules 'do not merely regulate, they create or define new forms of behaviour'. He goes on to suggest that chess is only possible with rules, but you can drive a car without knowing the road rules. Most concerns about banking are focused on the regulative kind of rules – questions of how we regulate banks better. Yet, it is the constitutive rules that actually matter most.

To elaborate, according to Searle constitutive rules operate where an activity depends on them for its existence; they are endogenous. Regulative rules, on the other hand, can be thought of as being exogenous; the activity in question does not depend on them. Expanding on Searle's framework, this means that the two types of rules operate on different levels of significance. To put it differently, regulative rules are rules of conduct such as those governing table manners, whereas constitutive rules are rules of purpose that constitute new identities and ideas. An important way to distinguish between these two types of rules and to establish if a rule is constitutive in character is by asking the question if a rule (be it a specific regulation or a broader principle) reshapes identity – in our case the identity of banks – or not. In this book we identify the shift in the self-identification of banks from market authorities to market players as an important constitutive rule change. Indeed, the mechanics of change work differently dependent on the rule at stake. With regard to

TABLE 1.2   A typology of rules

RULE TYPE	CONSTITUTIVE	REGULATIVE
Content	Creates or defines new forms of behaviour	Regulates antecedently or independently existing forms of behaviour
Level of significance	Endogenous: activity dependent on rule	Exogenous: activity independent of rule
Target	Rules of purpose	Rules of conduct
Rule change	Progressive or cumulative	Cyclical and linear; often simply repetitive
Examples	1933 Banking Act in the USA heralding era of 'repressed finance'	1988 Basel Capital Adequacy Accord setting minimum capital reserve requirements for internationally active banks

constitutive rules, change usually is progressive or cumulative. If we want to relate this to the preceding discussion, then the 1933 Banking Act in the United States and the era of 'repressed finance' that it heralded were such a constitutive rule change. In the case of regulative rules, change can be cyclical and linear and is often simply repetitive. Examples of this would be the 1988 Basel Accord that put into place minimum capital requirements for internationally active banks. This typology of rules is summarized in Table 1.2.

Bank regulation is underpinned by beliefs and norms that are only rarely articulated. Yet this is important because banking regulation as public policy is based on collective or intersubjective understandings that produce these constitutive rules. Especially with regard to the recent crisis, the dominant and, at least by some pundits, heavily criticized role attributed to public policy focused on its implication in the American mortgage crisis (see e.g. Tirole 2010: 47). Public policy as shaping the behaviour of banks in a much broader sense has largely escaped the attention it deserves. More specifically with regard to banking regulation, we suggest that, first, there has been growing emphasis on regulative over constitutive rules. This means that states have focused on designing rules for existing banking operations without paying due regard to what made this activity possible in the first place, or more profound considerations of what could and should count as legitimate banking activity.

Second, changes over the last three decades in government and financial markets, both domestically and globally, have fostered an increasingly synchronic (as opposed to diachronic) logic of banking practice and regulation. The synchronic refers originally in Saussure's writings to the internal logic of a language, and how the various elements coexist. A diachronic understanding of language considers the origins and processes of language development (Sinclair 2005: 58). As Cox notes, the synchronic approach to thought fits with the market mentality of profit maximization (Cox with Sinclair 1996: 188). The synchronic allows for the development of useful analytical frameworks such as value-at-risk, which banks use to assess the state of their books at any given period of time. The diachronic, or what Cox calls the 'time of duration', refers to much more complex social processes such as production. The neat deductive formulas of the synchronic mentality do not, argues Cox, fit the complexity of the diachronic (Cox with Sinclair 1996: 188). This means that, for example when it comes to investment, short-term profit maximization increasingly displaces investment in productive assets and capacity, over time running down those capacities (Sinclair 2005: 58–9).

These two trends have fundamentally changed the way that banks behave. The trajectories of these developments have been

FIGURE 1.1   Bank regulation and practice

LOGIC/BANK PRACTICE

	diachronic	synchronic
regulative	II	III
constitutive	I	IV

RULES/BANK REGULATION

highly uneven across the three regions under investigation in this book and across countries. Nevertheless, it would be wrong to focus solely on changes in financial markets to understand the problem with banks, given that, in recent decades, these were actually made possible or were compounded by changes in the regulatory approach. Figure 1.1 portrays the nature of the rules of bank regulation and the logic of banking practice along the diachronic–synchronic and constitutive–regulative axes.

The four quadrants depict possible constellations of the relationship between banking regulation and practice. Quadrant I combines a constitutive understanding of regulation with a diachronic approach to banking practice. Here, regulation is seen and practised in terms of the very foundations of what banks are. In terms of banking practice, long-term business relations trump short-term profit maximization. In this ideal-typical scenario, banks act as self-conscious market authorities. The outcome is a model of banking in which banks are aware of and pay tribute to their role as social actors. We can also call this the Jimmy Stewart model after his role in the movie *It's A Wonderful Life*. Stewart plays the owner of a savings-and-loan bank in small-town America. Stewart's character brings a halt to a run on the bank that would force it into bankruptcy and into the hands of a ruthless local rich man by telling his customers how their deposits fund houses and businesses owned by their neighbours, encouraging them to see their common interest. It is also approximated by the risk-sharing aspect of Islamic banking (Maurer 2005).

In quadrant II a regulative conception of regulation intersects with a diachronic logic of banking practice. Regulators focus on designing rules that constrain certain aspects of the way banks conduct their operations without directly interfering with their business decisions. Banks focus on long-term lending relationships and a stable depositor base. For a long time, the German banking model was held to be a close approximation of this ideal type (see e.g. Zysman 1983). Until 2005 *Landesbanken* were supported by state guarantees, making them more patient financiers than elsewhere. The end of these guarantees and the challenges this posed for their business models might also explain why some of these institutions became so heavily exposed to exactly those financial products that were at the heart of the global financial crisis.

In quadrant III a regulative understanding of regulation meets a synchronic logic of banking practice. Regulation is seen as being external to the way that banks operate. Banks 'play the market' and short-term profit maximization rules the day. This ideal-typical constellation is the opposite of the Jimmy Stewart banking model in quadrant I. As we will discuss in more detail in the subsequent chapters, what we have witnessed over the last decades is a strong push into this quadrant, ultimately giving rise to the global financial crisis.

Finally, quadrant IV represents the case where a constitutive approach to regulation coexists with a synchronic approach to bank operations. Regulation is constitutive in the sense that it defines what counts as permissible banking activity and what does not. However, banks make mainly short-term loans and lend for consumption rather than productive purposes. This might happen in countries where the political climate exhibits a degree of uncertainty that makes it unsafe for banks to enter long-term lending relationships. Consider, for example, the high proportion of short-term loans in many developing countries.

The existence of banks and their expanding role in everyday political, economic and socio-cultural life are highly contingent on government and the rules designed by it. We have to take into account not just the effects of banks on states (or perhaps rather their finances), but also the effects of states on banks. In this system, banks do not exist prior to states in a market utopia. States and banking have to be seen as being co-constitutive in a non-deterministic sense. States, however, act as perhaps the most important adjudicators and arbitrators of the norms underlying the regulation of banks. Nonetheless, changes in government as well as wider developments in financial markets have increasingly shifted regulatory practice and banking operations into the top right quadrant (III).

Banks are not constrained by regulation, they are made or constituted by it. In so doing, bank regulation also influences the logic according to which banks operate. Yet, if we think this through, to have any meaningful effect, bank regulation needs to address these constitutive foundations. It also must embrace diachronic elements about the purpose and time frame of banking. Regulation against the 'last' financial crisis is doomed to failure.

However, this means that we have to think more seriously about ways to move from the top right quadrant (III) to the bottom left quadrant (I).

This is the more important in the current situation, as we witness new regulation being drafted and enacted in response to the global financial crisis. As on previous occasions, policymakers perceive the design and implementation of new bank regulations as an important way to regain the confidence of financial markets and the general public. We suggest these efforts are likely to miss the point, if not exacerbate the situation. Our worry is that current reform proposals fail on at least one of the two fronts, by either reproducing a synchronic logic of banking practice or by focusing on designing regulative rules of conduct. Thus they have to be seen as falling into quadrants II–IV. The solution to tackling the problem with banks, however, lies in quadrant I.

There exist insurmountable tensions between the intended regulative rules of conduct discussed in policy circles (the dominant image of bank regulation in the mainstream literature and policymaking world) and banking regulation understood as a constitutive practice creating the banking activity it defines (the image of bank regulation put forward in this book). To come to terms with the problem with banks, we have to explore the role of bank regulation in the constitution of the entities it sets out to regulate. In recent discussions about how to reform the financial system through imposing new rules for banks, the mutually constitutive role played by banks and government regulation has been largely ignored. Yet, this relationship is critical when it comes to deliberating banking reform.

TWO

BANKING IS A CONFIDENCE GAME

In the cities of the developed world some of the best-kept and grandest buildings to be found are those belonging to banks. A walk through the financial district around Wall Street in Manhattan or the narrow streets of the City in London will reveal how wealth can be turned into bricks and mortar. The buildings in these places are constructed of the finest materials and are major architectural statements rather than of purely utilitarian design. Those banks built before World War II often resemble temples from classical antiquity. What you see is not accidental or merely the reflection of good business fortune. It is designed to impress upon the viewer how established, solid and permanent these banks are, to dispel any doubts the observer might have about the acumen of those behind the banks and their future prospects.

The long tradition of solid, expensive and perhaps anachronistic buildings in which you might be forgiven for expecting to find a Greek philosopher or a scene from a science-fiction movie are there to mask another, altogether less comforting, reality. As we saw in the last chapter, banking crises in the rich world are frequent and often deep. So it is no surprise that banks try to create an image of calm and collected activity, of probity and financial acumen. Banks have always faced major challenges and even the richest of them, such as investment bank Goldman Sachs, have come close to ruin in the right combination of circumstances, such as in 2008. When this happens we all suffer. Banks are not what they want you to think they are. What is interesting is how often we actually go along with the banks and accept their image of themselves despite the weight of historical experience.

This chapter sets out the first part of our case for thinking banking is a volatile and crisis-prone business with inherent problems that are much more significant than usually acknowledged. Most writers, while not suggesting banks and bankers are paragons of virtue, tend to blame external circumstances for the problems banks find themselves in from time to time. The global financial crisis that started in 2007 is no exception, with blame being attributed to subprime borrowers, the US government's promotion of housing as social policy, and the rise of China as a major creditor nation (Baker 2009). While 'greedy bankers' were subject to public vilification, and this remains an issue for banks, as we will discuss below, the properties of banks as institutions with particular motivations and pathologies were not part of the public debate. These pathologies are at the root of the problem with banks. However, what banks are and how they behave are not only a matter of their inherent properties. Importantly, we argue that banks are shaped in crucial ways by states and the rules and policies states impose on banks.

Contradictions

Banking is akin to a game of musical chairs. Citizens, businesses and governments circle the chairs while the music plays and all is well. But when the music stops and everyone runs towards the chairs it soon becomes clear that there are not enough chairs for everybody. Managing this contradiction by keeping the music playing is at the heart of banking. It is an intoxicating game, as Chuck Prince, CEO of Citigroup, suggested at the start of the global financial crisis when using a similar metaphor: 'As long as the music is playing, you've got to get up and dance' (quoted in Paulson 2010: 70). At the heart of this is the reality that banks are more than the strongrooms or counting houses of antiquity. Banks do not merely store money safely for their customers, as children imagine. In modern fractional reserve banking, banks pay interest on the funds deposited with them. In order to defray these liabilities, because that is what deposits are on bank balance sheets, banks lend money for which they charge borrowers interest. Banks do not keep a lot of money sitting in reserve waiting for depositors to make withdrawals. Banks typically keep less than 10 per cent in reserve. Most of the money deposited in the bank is lent out to earn an income for the bank, pay depositors, make up for bad debts and pay for the bank's overheads.

This looks like a good system. Savers put their money in the bank, the bank lends the money to people and companies that want to buy a house, a car or fund purchases of plant and equipment, and savers get rewarded with interest. No doubt the credit this supplies is vital to the standard of living we enjoy. Economists celebrate this as a broadly efficient system. But there is a problem in this arrangement. Bank loans are, from the point of view of the bank, illiquid. They run over long periods of time. But depositors can withdraw their demand deposits without notice. This maturity mismatch, combined with the fact that banks have little cash on hand in the form of reserves, makes banks vulnerable to any news that gives rise to a sudden demand by a large number of depositors for their funds. This maturity mismatch results from the gap between the synchronic logic of deposits, where depositors are free to seek the best return for their cash, with no notice, and the diachronic or time-bound social relationship of borrowing, in which those who are lent sums by the bank are bound to the bank until the loan is repaid or otherwise liquidated. Banks manage this contradiction at the core of their business, but when management ceases to be effective the contradiction can become manifest and threaten the existence of the bank.

The failure to manage what amounts to the contradiction between the synchronic interests of depositors and the diachronic relationship of borrowers can give rise to some nasty events, as the global financial crisis that started in 2007 has demonstrated. In a bank run, such as occurred in the case of British bank Northern Rock in September 2007, rumours began to circulate about the health of the bank after it approached the Bank of England in August seeking liquidity support. In the first run on a British bank in over a hundred years, lines of depositors formed outside branches seeking withdrawal of their funds. Subsequently, the bank was nationalized. An essential point about a bank run is that even if the stories about the solvency of a bank are false, immediate demands from depositors have a self-fulfilling effect because they can make the bank insolvent as most of the bank's funds have been lent to borrowers. The uncertainty and fear represented by the bank run can have even bigger effects. Banks and other financial institutions must have confidence in each other and the system as a whole to transact with each other, just as members of other communities must trust in the parties they are transacting with. Unlike other markets, financial ones often involve few tangible assets that can be liquidated if things go wrong, so confidence in counter-parties is essential. This broke down catastrophically in 2007–09, in what Wessel has called the 'Great Panic', Germain the 'Great Freeze' and others a valuation crisis (Wessel 2009: 1; Germain 2010: 79; Sinclair 2010b: 101).

Banks and other institutions were unwilling to buy and sell securities from each other because the panic over subprime assets that started in the summer of 2007 meant they were uncertain about the financial condition of other institutions. This effectively stopped the markets in their tracks for a time. A third consequence of the failure to manage the contradiction between synchronic and diachronic features of banking is more subtle. It involves the loss of confidence in banking as a cornerstone of capitalist society among the generation who experience a combination of bank runs and valuations crises. The generation of the 1930s experienced this loss of confidence like the present generation.

Social Foundations

Bank runs, the Great Freeze and the bank legitimacy crisis show that banking is a social phenomenon, and we argue that the implications of the social character of banking are crucial to understanding the problem with banks. But banking is not usually understood in these terms but rather as a natural thing. This is the view of the exogenous approach to finance (Sinclair 2010b). This tradition's modern founders include Hayek and Friedman. Their views are associated with attacks on the model of state intervention popular in much of the developed world after the Great Depression of the 1930s. These thinkers took it as axiomatic that markets, when left to their own devices, are efficient allocators of resources. For them, financial crisis is a deviation from the normal state of the market. Given they assume markets and institutions like banks work efficiently, this tradition focuses on 'external' causes, especially government failure, as the cause of problems. Friedman, for example, blamed the Great Depression of the 1930s on what he considered to be incorrect Federal Reserve policy in 1929 and 1930, rather than the effects of the stock-market crash in October 1929 (Kindleberger and Aliber, 2005: 72).

Exogenous accounts assume market participants like banks are constantly adjusting their behaviour – for example, whether they buy or sell financial instruments like bonds and stocks – based on new information from outside the market. In this context, market prices always reflect what other market participants are prepared to pay. If this is the case, reason exogenous thinkers, prices are never inflated or false. They must always be correct. So the idea of a 'bubble economy', in which assets like houses, stocks and oil futures deviate from true value to a higher, false value, is rejected. There can be no 'true value' other than what the market is prepared to pay. This Efficient Markets Hypothesis (EMH) is central to the exogenous view of crises. In the EMH, prices for stocks, bonds, derivatives and so on are always based on all the available information. They therefore reflect the fundamental value of these securities. Real-world markets are efficient in that securities trade at equilibrium between supply and demand. It is a remarkable claim about information and how it is incorporated into market prices.

How does the EMH argument work? The case for EMH is built on three claims. First, investors are said to be rational and to value their potential purchases rationally. So investors are not likely to buy before finding out about what they are buying and thinking about how to maximize their return. Second, if there are irrational investors their random trades will cancel each other out, leaving prices unaffected. Irrationality is the exception and it is of no consequence. Last, even if there is a consistently ir-rational approach to investing among a group of investors, based on phases of the moon for example, rational arbitrageurs will meet them in the market and eliminate their influence on prices, based on asserting fundamental values.

What are the implications of the EMH for financial markets? First, asset prices for stocks and bonds incorporate all information, providing very accurate signals to buyers and sellers. If this is correct, asset price bubbles are simply not possible. Second, there is 'no free lunch', because traders cannot beat the market. If everyone in the market has the information, any cheap or expensive assets will be rapidly identified by traders, and arbitraged away. Just as it is difficult to beat the house at roulette, it is hard to beat the market under these assumptions.

What are the problems with EMH? In Paul Davidson's words, EMH holds that the future is 'merely the statistical shadow of the past' (Davidson quoted in Sinclair 2009). In other words, financial economists calculate probable future risks based on historical data. Unfortunately, human societies are not, in the words of Robert Skidelsky, 'a stable and repetitive universe' (quoted in Sinclair 2009). Communities are more like living things than automobile engines. They grow, change, adjust and over time are transformed. They are non-linear. Adopting a fundamental axiom more appropriate for the physical world than the social world seems like a bad start for the banks.

Eliminating the idea of uncertainty from the lexicon of the developed financial markets has been problematic. EMH encourages much confidence in financial engineering. If more of our financial activities assumed a level of uncertainty, and therefore we would have to be more risk-averse, we would live in a world of more conservatively managed banks, companies, governments and individuals. Of course, the trade-off would be a society more like that of our grandparents, in which getting a mortgage was a struggle and the general economic standard of living was lower. But the global financial crisis has forcibly re-created that world for a good portion now in any case. The exogenous world-view has encouraged developed markets to neglect the regulation of key institutions like banks that actually make markets work. EMH encourages neglect of the role of institutions like banks because it says that information works to impose automatically the discipline of the market, rather like an operating system in a computer. But in a non-linear world institutions are fundamental to instilling confidence in market participants about the future. In an uncertain world we need institutions we feel we can trust in order to engage in financial transactions.

The endogenous account says we must look inside banks for trouble. For Marx and Polanyi, banking crises are caused by the internal 'laws of motion' of the capitalist mode of production. These produce constant change and upheaval, not equilibrium between demand and supply. For Keynes, the 'animal spirits' or passions of speculation give rise to risky activities by banks and other financial institutions. Typical of the endogenous perspective is the idea that market traders do not merely integrate information coming from outside the markets in the wider, real economy, but are focused on what other traders are doing, in an effort to anticipate their buy/sell activities, and thus make money from them (or at least avoid losing more money than the market average). Given this, rumours, norms and other features of social life are part of their understanding of how finance works. On this account, banks and finance more broadly are subject to the pathologies of social life, like any other activity in which humans engage. This is an image of finance far from the self-regulating conception that characterizes the exogenous view and far from the image bankers cultivate of themselves.

Keynes provided what remains perhaps the best intuitive illustration of the importance of the necessity of this internal, social understanding of banking and finance in his tabloid beauty contest metaphor, first published in 1936 (Akerlof and Shiller 2009: 133). Keynes suggested that the essence of banking and finance is not, as most supposed, a matter of picking the best financial products, based on economic and financial analysis. Anticipating what other bankers and traders in the financial markets were likely to do next was actually more relevant. Keynes compared banking and finance to beauty contests that ran in the popular newspapers of his time. These contests were not, as might be assumed, about picking the most attractive face. Success was achieved by estimating how other readers would vote and voting with them, although, as Keynes pointed out, others would be trying to do the same, hence the complexity and volatility of financial markets and the challenges faced by banks.

The social foundations of banking highlighted by Keynes are similar to those we find at the heart of a bank run. This is the reality that the significance of banks is not like a mountain, a 'brute' fact which is true (or not) irrespective of shared beliefs about its existence; nor are the 'subjective' facts of individual perception important, other than to the individual (Searle 2005). What is central to banking and the problems of banks is what people believe about banks, and act on collectively – even if those beliefs prove subsequently to be false. Indeed, the beliefs may be quite strange to the observer, but if people use them as a guide to action (or inaction) they are significant. Dismissing these collective beliefs as false neglects the consequentiality of social facts.

States, Rules and Crisis

As we noted in the first chapter, Searle helps us understand that collectively shared ideas are not ephemeral but material to the problem of banks. Most concerns about banking are focused on the regulative kind of rules – questions of how we regulate banks better. The public and elite panic in the West surrounding the global financial crisis focused on regulative rules and those who allegedly broke them. But this is not what brought about the Great Panic or the global financial crisis. Constitutive rules, the basic social foundations of market interaction such as trust and confidence in transactions, were seriously damaged. This is why the crisis was so deep and so obviously challenging to the major banks in developed markets.

So far we have argued that banking is an inherently fraught business because the logic of banking is founded on a contradiction between synchronic depositors and diachronic borrowers. Banks manage this contradiction, and when they mess it up bank runs, 'great freezes' and legitimacy crises tend to follow. But these claims have been made in abstraction from the major source of governance in our world. Governments, as anyone who has observed banks in recent years knows, are key players in the world of finance. But, unlike those who write about finance and banks in the exogenous school, we argue that governments are not just regulative rule makers who ensure banks are sticking to rules that make the markets fair and are good for consumers. We agree that states are key players in the maintenance and reproduction of the regulative rules that help bankers manage the contradictions at the heart of their business. At the same time, more fundamentally, governments reproduce the system of constitutive rules that makes banking possible in the first place. When the system falls into crisis, as it did in the 1930s and again starting in 2007, states are willing to throw out whatever limits they may have placed on themselves, and do what is necessary, such as serving as lender of last resort, to make sure the system is rebooted and banks can get back to business. Our point is that the problem of banks is not natural, or just market-derived. Banks only function because the deeper set of rules that allow them to exist in the first place is built and reproduced for them by governments. As states have become more dependent on bank financing of their wars, economic development and welfare through the years, they have taken more interest in the fundamentals that make banking possible: the integrity of the currency, weights and measures, the protection of property, the sanctity of contracts, bookkeeping standards.

Banking crises of the sort we have known in recent years are a reflection of a breakdown in constitutive rules, in which states are heavily implicated. Banking crises are shocking events. Typically, big, shattering crises occur after long periods of affluent self-confidence. Pride comes before the fall. The reversal they represent seems incomprehensible to those at the centre of things, never mind the general public. Typical of each episode are efforts to identify villains, often several, who can be held responsible for the crisis. Seemingly extravagant bankers' bonuses are a recent example. This pattern is evident in the event which set the standard against which all financial crises are measured: the Great Depression of the 1930s. At the height of the Depression a quarter of American workers were unemployed (Galbraith 1997: 168). The New York Stock Exchange did not return to its summer 1929 level until the early 1950s, almost a quarter-century after the crash of October 1929 (Dow Jones 2009).

As we discussed in the previous chapter, financial crises did not, however, start in the twentieth century. The Dutch 'tulip mania' of the 1630s, in which tulip bulbs dramatically appreciated in value, is usually cited as the first boom and bust in tradable assets. At the time, tulips were exotic imports from the eastern Mediterranean. 'Mass mania' for the bulbs led to massive price inflation in these assets, as in a stock market boom, making bulbs worth the equivalent of US$50,000 or more each. When the crash came and the bubble deflated 'not with a whimper but with a bang', many who had invested their life savings in

FIGURE 2.1   International capital mobility and episodes of banking
crisis 1800–2008

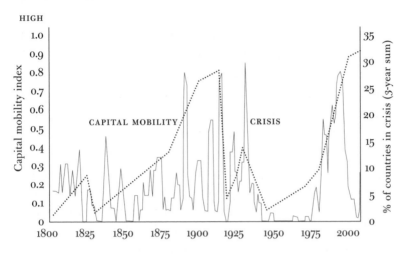

Source: Reinhart and Rogoff 2008: 23, 58–61.

tulips lost everything (Galbraith 1993: 4). Mass default ensured
a depression in the Netherlands in the years after 1637 (Galbraith
1993: 26–33). Nevertheless, as Figure 2.1 shows, banking crises
became more common throughout the course of the nineteenth
century as fractional reserve banking – with its prerequisite of
strong confidence in the banks – spread and international capital
mobility increased, making it easier for crises to be transmitted
from one country to another. What is also remarkable about the
trends portrayed in this figure is the nearly complete absence of
banking crises from the 1940s to the late 1970s, a time during
which international capital mobility was low as well.

Indeed, the link between greater international capital mobility
and the frequency and severity of banking crises should not
be ignored. In the wake of the 1930s' banking crisis, American

policymakers put into place reforms that put severe restrictions on the ways in which banks could operate: the 1933 Banking Act of the previous chapter. However, they also undertook collective efforts on the international level to insulate domestic financial systems from international capital flows and thus to give themselves the domestic policy space for their banking reforms to work. After the Great Depression and World War II, the Bretton Woods regime – a system of constitutive rules for monetary affairs on a global scale – was created to bring greater order to the international monetary system. As much a political as an economic framework, Bretton Woods was intended to avoid rapid and unsettling economic adjustments within countries. The hope was that this would avoid the sort of economic problems which contributed to World War II, and which would, some feared, increase support for the communist system in the Soviet Union.

Bretton Woods had been created at the end of 1944 and was a key element in the effort to build a multilateral economic system. It facilitated the balancing of liabilities between countries without the need for states to deflate their economies, putting people out of work. A contraction in economic activity had been the usual way in which countries adjusted to each other during the era of the gold standard prior to World War I. The architects of Bretton Woods saw this adjustment process as politically impossible after World War II, given the heightened expectations of returning soldiers and their families for a good, secure life. The planners were also keen to avoid the return of destabilizing capital flows between societies, which they blamed for the financial volatility, banking crises and trade friction between the wars. Although the intent behind Bretton Woods was to avoid crises and the political conflict that followed, despite US assistance it had relatively few resources at its disposal. Given the considerable protectionism in trade which followed the war, countries were frequently either in sizeable surplus or deficit in their national accounts. Whilst the Bretton Woods system certainly was not as stable as its myth suggests, given that liquidity creation was premissed upon the United States incurring a balance-of-payments deficit which in the long run would undermine the credibility of the US dollar as its anchor currency (Triffin 1961), for the purpose of this book it was nevertheless an important era as it was characterized by the near absence of banking crises, at least in the developed world.

The system provided a protective environment for banks that during this time largely focused on their domestic operations. Barriers to entry were high. Competition was limited by regulation that also served to 'pad' the profits of banks (Rosenbluth and Schaap 2003). For example, in the United States restrictions on the interest paid on demand deposits prevented banks from competing excessively with each other for business. However, the implicit cost of this system was borne by borrowers, who had to pay more for loans, and depositors, who received less income on their deposits. Whole groups of society were precluded from taking out loans. The safety of deposits was a key priority in this system, even though it came at a cost to consumers. In so doing, government regulation was constitutive of the way that banks operated. As Rosenbluth and Schaap (2003: 311) suggest, '[p]rofit padding works because that very profitability disinclines banks to take undue risks.' Similar regulations were in place in Japan and in Germany and in many other countries. Product innovation was tightly controlled. Seeking higher margins, there was a trend of American banks venturing abroad that began to gather speed in the late 1950s and gave new impetus to the development of the Euromarkets in the City of London. Slowly, the protective domestic frameworks for banks that had been developed since the 1930s and that had been safeguarded with the arrangements set in place in Bretton Woods in 1944 were undermined.

With the demise of this system, banking had to face a more volatile world. The Bretton Woods system of fixed exchange rates and controls over the movement of capital was gradually abandoned in the fifteen years after 1970, and so were many of the more prescriptive rules that applied to banks in advanced industrialized countries, such as caps on interest rates and selective credit controls (Rosenbluth and Schaap 2003; Kane 1977). What emerged was a new system of constitutive rules orchestrated by states that provided the context for banks and financial institutions in which floating exchange rates were increasingly the norm, at least in developed countries, and in which capital could flow freely around the world to sources of highest return. The end of Bretton Woods, and the re-emergence of global finance in the 1970s and 1980s, characterized by increasingly free capital movements, created significant problems, and, as Figure 2.1 shows, banking crises became once more a concern.

Volatility, especially in exchange rates, was an issue in the 1970s and 1980s. The 1980s were marked by a major debt crisis involving bank lending to developing countries, mostly in Latin America, and a series of currency crises, as the values of major currencies like the Japanese yen appreciated, causing trouble for trade partners. Perhaps the most dramatic of these events was the Exchange Rate Mechanism crisis of 1992, in which currency traders, most famously George Soros, placed bets on the ability of the British government to keep the pound sterling within the European Exchange Rate Mechanism (ERM), despite much higher inflation and interest rates in Britain than in the major ERM countries such as Germany. After spending £3.3 billion defending the pound the British government had to abandon the defence of sterling, which exited the ERM. Europeans in particular were concerned about the negative implications of floating currencies. For them, the attractions of a more ordered world were very strong.

This is not to say that during this period states did not attempt to regulate banks. Indeed, the Basel Accord of 1988, requiring banks to hold a minimum capital reserve of 8 per cent, was a significant step with regard to the international coordination of banking regulation. However, they lacked the ambition of their predecessors at Bretton Woods. Moreover, there was a shift in the understood purpose of financial regulation from being market constraining to being market enhancing. We return to this point in Chapter 4. The 1980s were also a time in which cooperation between rich country central banks became increasingly formalized. Although a floating exchange rate regime should rapidly adjust to reflect the changing economic conditions in a country (real interest rates, inflation, profit margins, regulations, political stability), this proved less than perfect.

The Asian financial crisis of 1997/98 was the culmination of a boom in Asia that led to what in hindsight turned out to be excessive short-term lending and risky pegging of national currencies to the US dollar, a problem also for Argentina in 2001. As in Holland in the 1630s, the result of the crisis was economic depression in some countries, notably Indonesia, where the price of basic foodstuffs and other costs increased dramatically. The Asian crisis, like the financial crisis that began in 2007, led to accusations of lax regulation, fraud and corruption. The rapid reversal of portfolio investment flows out of these countries led to the collapse of national banking systems. In Malaysia, despite a barrage of Western criticism, controls on the movement of capital were reintroduced, challenging what were the prevailing neo-liberal constitutive rules, until the market panic eased. With the Asian crisis it became clear that the ideal of a smoothly functioning financial system is far from an accomplished fact. However, with time, as was the case with prior crises, the motivation to reform and control volatility subsided and efforts to create a 'new international financial architecture' stalled. This was despite similar types of crisis occurring in Mexico in the mid-1990s and again in a range of countries in the late 1990s (e.g. Russia, Brazil) and early 2000s (e.g. Argentina, Uruguay).

During this time, the developed world also had its fair share of crises. Whilst they were not banking crises in the definition used by Reinhart and Rogoff and on which Figure 2.1 is based (they were not bank runs, nor did they represent the taking over of a bank into administration), the analyst scandals of the early 2000s and the collapse of a series of companies, ranging from Enron in the United States to Parmalat in Italy, showed that banks were less able to manage conflicts of interest than they claimed they were (Palazzo and Rethel 2008). However, legislation that was enacted in response to the Enron debacle, namely the Sarbanes–Oxley Act signed into effect by George W. Bush in 2002, was largely regulative in nature, failing to embrace the social foundations of banking and the constitutive role of regulation.

What unites the Enron and Parmalat scandals with the sub-prime events of 2007–09 is the important role of extreme forms of financial innovation. Enron, a Texas-based energy company, had used multiple special-purpose vehicles to keep highly leveraged activities off balance sheet with the connivance of auditor Arthur Andersen. Parmalat, with the help of its banks and auditors, managed to accrue a debt of 14.3 billion hidden via special-purpose vehicles, which ultimately led to its collapse in 2003 (BBC News, 26 January 2004). Citigroup, which had helped Parmalat to set up a special-purpose vehicle, tellingly called Buconero (black hole) LLC, was later exonerated (*New York Times*, 20 October 2008). (Previously it had reached settlements over its involvement with Enron and WorldCom.) In the case of the subprime crisis, securities were created out of underlying loans to residential mortgage borrowers with relatively weak personal credit ratings.

The holders of these securities had little understanding of the quality of the underlying assets. With the advantage of hindsight it is clear, as the Bank of England notes, that this involved an implicit underpricing of risk (Bank of England 2007: 5). What distinguishes subprime from Enron and Parmalat, and makes subprime much more of a systemic threat, is not innovation itself but the corrosive effect of market uncertainty on all valuations in the securities market by all institutions. The whole system was affected. It was easy to dismiss Enron as a gang of bad guys engaging in illegal market manipulation. But the essence of the subprime crisis is not illegality or even the bankruptcy of the working poor, but uncertainty about the financial engineering at the heart of the global banking system, and the fragility this uncertainty creates.

One of the realities of global politics is that the most important things are often overshadowed by what, on a dispassionate analysis, are really much less significant issues. This is most unfortunate because it means that what is happening in the 'engine room' of globalization is often poorly understood by those in power and by those who wish to change the policies of those in power. Much of this neglect can be explained by the mythic technical character of finance, especially as it is talked about by business people, and written about by many journalists, government officials and even some scholars. Finance and money are discussed as if they are purely technical matters that those without the requisite training cannot hope to understand. The widespread propagation and acceptance of this falsehood makes it easy for those with policy control to pursue their objectives without informed democratic debate.

The usual claim made about the securitization process in the developed financial markets is that it led to a breakdown in the relationship between the originators of mortgages and those in the financial markets creating and trading in the bonds and derivatives that pooled the stream of income from these mortgages. Because people in the financial markets were so distant from the actual credit risk of the individual mortgage payers and may have been poorly advised by credit rating agencies, they underestimated the riskiness of the assets (Sinclair 2005). This meant the financial system was full of 'toxic assets'; once this was fully appreciated by markets in the summer of 2007 as a result of increasing mortgage defaults by subprime borrowers, panic developed, followed by the collapse of a number of major financial institutions, worldwide government intervention to prop up the markets, and the subsequent recession. Popular accounts such as Baker's assert that too much debt was accumulated, and that therefore it was inevitable that the boom would collapse into bust (Baker 2009). The standard account of the crisis suggests that it occurred because some people were not doing their jobs properly, and that, if we can just make sure people do what they are supposed to, another financial crisis like this can be avoided. In this account Asia avoided crisis because the region did not have the financial engineering characteristic of the West.

The substantive problem that generated the global financial crisis was not extreme financial engineering as such, but a breakdown in the social foundations that underpin transactions. The breakdown happened to be localized in the main metropolitan centres of global finance, especially New York and London, where financial innovation was most extreme, leaving trust and confidence largely unaffected in some other places, including most of Asia. The most prominent symptom of this social crisis was the valuation crisis known as the Great Panic or Great Freeze, in which banks became unwilling to trade with each other or lend money. Subprime problems merely served as the tripwire to this panic. Other bad news might have had the same effect on the markets, as Galbraith shows is typical at the top of a financial boom (Galbraith 1993: 4).

It does us no favours to see banks as smoothly oiled machines we damage through aberrant use. Sentiment, as a bank run illustrates, is key to whether banks and financial markets work for us or not, and sentiment is volatile. This crisis happened because sentiment was excited. The confidence in financial markets had, prior to 2007, reached such a frenzy that it had become an episode of 'irrational exuberance', like so many financial manias before. As Henry Paulson makes clear, this confidence was so strong that even uninsured money-market funds run by investment banks made returns as if they were insured by deposit insurance (Paulson 2010: 235). The 'bad news' about subprime lending was actually quite modest in summer 2007, but in the context of the preceding mania this was enough to serve as the tripwire and cause panic. The panic created widespread uncertainty about the quality of the balance sheets of banks. It is this uncertainty that effectively brought the financial markets to a halt, forcing government intervention.

Conclusion

Banks do not work as we think they do. They function with the ever-present threat of being overwhelmed by their contradictions. Managing those contradictions is a tough job. When the assumptions that underpin that management come apart – as happened in the 1930s and again in 2007–09 – confidence is lost, bank runs occur and financial paralysis may set in. States are actively involved in this confidence game. Governments provide the infrastructure of laws and institutions which support transactions. In times of crisis, states typically stand ready to play the role of lender of last resort to support or restore market confidence.

Given the negative impact on banks of the Lehmann bankruptcy in mid-September 2008, at least as it was felt at the time, the necessity of this state role in supporting the constitutive rules for banks seems clearer than ever.

Banks are much more social creatures than most people think. Understanding banks is not about brute facts. The values on a balance sheet are dependent upon confidence, and when an institution is in trouble those values are quite different from the figures when the institution is thought to be doing well. So value is dependent on confidence, which is a social fact rather than a material property. States are active agents in the construction and maintenance of that confidence. States try to paper over the contradictions of banking by using devices such as deposit insurance and playing the role of lender of last resort. Both these means may perversely encourage banks to be reckless, knowing governments will bail them and their customers out should the worst happen. At the same time states have exposed banks to competition and pushed them towards a more synchronic form, reproducing the problem with banks and pushing banks towards crisis. The next chapter considers the broader context in which banks operate and the impact this has had on financial innovation and risk-taking in banking.

THREE

DISINTERMEDIATION
AND FINANCIAL INNOVATION

Despite the effort to generate a calm exterior, banks are institutions under a lot of pressure, perhaps now more than ever. Broad
structural change has transformed the commercial environment
and opened up new possibilities for bank customers. Until the
1990s, most businesses outside the United States that wanted to
borrow money had to go to a bank. Barriers to entry were high
and banking was a relatively cosy business. This gave banks a
great deal of power and made them more than just market entities. Until this time, banks were really semi-public authorities,
in the sense that they had the ability to grant or deny credit
to whole categories of business. Their customers treated them
accordingly, rather than just as sellers of goods in the market,
like any other. This structure of privilege and authority has been
challenged by the increased competitive pressures generated by
the liberalization and deregulation of markets in the developed
world since the end of the Bretton Woods system. This change
has put a premium on the cost of financing, which has made
what banks traditionally did look expensive and encouraged
alternative forms of finance, changing banks themselves in the
process.

Liberalization, although reflecting policy choices rather than a natural, inevitable process and thus a product of government, has a discernible logic of its own. That logic has put pressure on the institutional model of traditional bank intermediation, in which banks undertook the maturity transformation of deposits into loans. This has not meant the end of banks, but we argue it has changed their identity and behaviour dramatically as these institutions attempt to survive in this very different world. The constitutive rules underpinning banking have changed, encouraged by liberalization, and these new rules have made banking more market-based and synchronic. It is a great irony that this struggle to survive by banks, which triggered the astonishing tidal wave of financial innovation evident in the past decade, ended up threatening the very existence of the banking industry that promoted it in the first place. This demonstrates that for all the weaknesses of banks as institutions, they remain in a strategic position to do systemic damage to global finance and society.

Sources and Signs of Change

As we saw in the last chapter, after the Great Depression and World War II, the Bretton Woods system was created to bring greater order to the global financial system. The constitutive rules ushered in by the Bretton Woods system were diachronic in nature, premised on the view that the mobility of capital created volatility in the foreign exchange market, which tended to disrupt imports and exports, throwing people out of work and creating the basis for social unrest and political upheaval. So the system was focused on facilitating free trade in goods but repressing financial markets and making them serve trade, rather than on allowing finance to become an international industry in its own right. However, Keynes's idea of controlling not just capital outflows but also capital inflows was not enacted as part of the Bretton Woods system in the face of opposition from the New York financial community. In the 1950s, once full currency convertibility had been re-established, the British government sought ways to expand the international business of the City of London, and restore to it the role of international financial centre the City had enjoyed before the First World War. By freeing international finance from domestic regulation and control, the British government played a key role in attracting footloose capital and creating a place where banks could operate under less 'repressive' conditions. Governments themselves were central to the erosion of the Bretton Woods system, not just banks or other financial institutions.

The 1960s was a period of high economic growth and a bull market in finance. US corporations expanded their activities abroad and used the international markets such as the City of London to finance their activities and avoid US rules such as Regulation Q, which banned interest payments on current or demand accounts. The Vietnam War and the Great Society welfare programmes initiated by President Johnson dominated US federal spending during this decade, financed by printing money rather than through austerity. This massively expanded the supply of US dollars and increased inflation, challenging the premisses of the Bretton Woods system, based on convertibility of dollars into gold. The United States 'closed the gold window' in 1971, taking the dollar off gold, eliminating any tangible basis to international liquidity. International money, like banking, became dependent purely on confidence. Governments were more important than ever in maintaining this confidence.

In 1973 the renewed Arab–Israeli conflict led to a quadrupling in the price of oil as Arab states demonstrated their anger at Western support for Israel. This highly disruptive event channelled large revenues to oil-producing states, which they deposited with rich country banks, creating a challenge for these banks. As we have seen, deposits are liabilities on bank balance sheets. So banks had incentives to find productive ways to lend out these petrodollars. Inevitably, this led to a lowering of credit standards. Many of the borrowers of these funds were developing countries which might otherwise have been forced to seek funds from the International Monetary Fund and the World Bank. They were delighted to obtain funds from private sources without the usual official scrutiny. Banks had lent these funds at floating rates and so were making a good return in excess of inflation. Unfortunately, when the US Federal Reserve under Chairman Paul Volcker shifted policy in 1979 to reduce inflation in the United States, interest rates rose dramatically and global commodity prices fell as the USA entered a bitter recession. These movements rapidly put the heavily leveraged developing countries into difficulty as their outgoings soared to meet borrowing costs, but their incomes collapsed as prices and the sales volume of their goods fell. Mexico was the first country to default in 1982, followed by others, including Argentina and Brazil, leading to a 'lost decade' in Latin America. Western banks avoided insolvency because Western governments aided debtor states to restructure and repay their obligations. The Latin American debt crisis demonstrated that banks were no longer tied to the repressed financial conditions of Bretton Woods. They needed to lend money and they would fit their lending standards to the circumstances rather than what was traditionally regarded as prudent. Equally, the event showed that government had to play a central role in making this volatile system viable for the banks.

Financial innovation accelerated after the Bretton Woods era of financial repression ended in the early 1970s. Investment banks offered money market funds to offer depositors higher returns on their ready cash, without the deposit insurance that had applied to US bank deposits since the 1930s. A high-yield (or junk bond) market emerged in the late 1970s, based in part on the work of Michael Milken, formerly of Drexel Burnham Lambert, the major Wall Street investment bank. Milken's arguments about capital access and the credit rating system, and his activities as the 'junk bond king' during the 'junk bond decade' of the late 1970s to late 1980s, remain the subject of considerable dispute (Stein 1992). During his graduate education at the Wharton School in Philadelphia, Milken read Hickman's work on returns in the bond market (Hickman 1958). Hickman claimed that low-grade or junk bonds promised high yields when held in large numbers in a diversified portfolio. Hickman suggested that these returns more than compensated for the additional default risk of the lower-rated debt (Hickman 1958: 26). According to Bailey, Milken formed the view that ratings had over time 'become moral absolutes' among investors (Bailey 1991: 25). Following Hickman, Milken observed that downgraded bonds 'were held in more contempt by investors than they deserved to be' (Bailey 1991: 25). Like some of the investment writers of the time, Milken, Bailey claims, saw that the primary problem with the ratings process was that it was too focused on past performance. However, bonds were obligations for future payment, and even a 'AAA' rating was 'no guarantee' that change would not intervene and cause a default (Bailey 1991: 26).

According to Toffler, Milken the investment banker can best be interpreted as attempting to establish a new order in the financial industry, which, as Toffler saw it, was 'hidebound and protected', and a 'major barrier to change', in which only smokestack, blue-chip industrial 'dinosaurs' could get long-term investment capital, because the two rating services 'guarded the gates of capital' (Toffler 1990: 44–7). As Toffler observed, conflict between those who wanted to 'restrict access to capital so that they themselves could control it', and those like Milken, who supposedly sought a 'democratization of capital', has a long history in the United States and elsewhere (Toffler 1990: 49–50). Whatever we think of Milken's motivations, the result of the initiative of Milken and others, as Grant, publisher of *Grant's Interest Rate Observer*, has noted, was that the 'marginal borrower received the benefit of the doubt' from the American banking industry in the 1980s (Grant 1992: 437). This tendency threatened to foster an 'emerging power structure' that would change the 'game', as Grant put it (Grant 1992: 393). The broader movement to weaken credit standards posed a challenge to established relationships on Wall Street and in corporate America. Within ten years at Drexel, Milken had raised US$93 billion, and the junk bond market had grown to US$200 billion, serving over 1,500 companies (Yago 1991: 25).

Congressional testimony revealed opposition to what some credit rating agency officials called the 'extreme financial leverage' attributable to junk bond financing of leveraged-buy-outs in the late 1980s. Bachmann, a senior executive at Standard & Poor's, emphasized probable constraints on innovation, and the tendency of managers to sell assets and skimp on strategic planning under such heavy debt loads (Bachmann 1990: 13). Grant cast the net wider in his testimony. As he saw things, in the 1980s 'every American with a mailbox was invited to borrow' (Grant 1990: 18). He blamed this 'explosion of the credit supply' on 'the long-standing tendency toward the socialization of credit risk that had its roots in the reforms of the early 1930s'. Milken had to be understood, Grant implied, in terms of a profligate US government whose net worth in 1988 was negative US$2.5 trillion (Grant 1990: 22). However, from the current vantage point it is important to emphasize that 1980s' financial innovations such as junk bonds mainly contributed to an expansion of corporate debt; the explosion of personal debt that was made so visible by the subprime crisis was yet to occur.

Rise of the Capital Markets

So far in this chapter we have discussed the relaxation in lending standards and financial innovation that followed the collapse of the Bretton Woods system. Governments and banks together helped bring about this process of change. Underlying all this was the reality that bank intermediation is a very particular and costly way of raising capital. The way in which wholesale borrowers obtain funds has been changing. Traditionally, borrowers have sought funds from banks. Banks obtained funds from depositors and lent this money out at a premium above the interest they paid. The bank made the decisions and assumed the risk that the borrower would repay on time with interest. If the borrower failed to repay, depositors were not directly affected, unless, of course, repayment problems were endemic across the bank's borrowers, placing the bank as a whole in financial jeopardy. Even these risks were lessened by regulation such as the Glass–Steagall Act of 1933, which prevented American commercial banks from underwriting the issue of securities such as bonds and led to the creation of the Federal Deposit Insurance Corporation, which guaranteed depositors' money in member institutions up to certain limits (Downes and Goodman, 1991: 173, 139). These constitutive measures were attempts to inject more predictability into economic affairs in response to the Great Depression, and were copied in various forms around the world (Polanyi 1957). Outside the United States, the dominance of banks in the business of lending funds has been more pronounced, as pointed out by Zysman (1983).

Zysman identified three sets of financial arrangements. The first of these is what he called the capital market form, characterized by competitive price allocation, arm's-length relations between government and industry, company-led adjustment and the absence of conscious development strategy. The second form, the credit-based system with government-administered prices, was designed to facilitate government intervention and state-led adjustment. The last system Zysman discussed was a variant on the credit-based system of capital allocation, in which financial institutions use market power to influence industrial investment decisions by corporations. Zysman saw the United States as the classic example of the first system, Japan and France as exemplifying the second, and Germany as an expression of the third (Zysman 1983: 18). These ideal types are no longer wholly accurate accounts of the way capital is allocated. The 1980s and 1990s saw a dynamic of disintermediation unleashed upon the markets for capital. This has changed the role of banks and heightened the importance of other institutions in capital allocation, at the same time changing the very nature of banks themselves.

What is disintermediation and why has it occurred? Disintermediation is a process of eliminating the 'middleman'. It has occurred on both sides of the balance sheet. Depositors have found better things to do with their funds at the same time as borrowers have increasingly been obtaining funds from sources other than borrowing from banks. The process accelerated in the 1990s and 2000s. In the USA alone, mutual funds, which sweep depositors' money directly into securities and money markets, contained US$11.8 trillion in assets in 2010, considerably more than the US$7.9 trillion held in US bank deposits (Investment Company Institute 2011: ii; FDIC 2011). Moreover, this trend has not been restricted to the United States alone. Globally, mutual fund assets are estimated to stand at close to US$25 trillion at the time of writing (Investment Company Institute 2011: 187). Currently, 44 per cent of American households own mutual funds, a massive increase from 6 per cent in 1980 (Investment Company Institute 2011: ii; *The Economist* 1994: 11). The shift on the borrowing side is just as marked. In 1970, commercial lending by banks made up 65 per cent of the borrowing needs of corporate America (*The Economist*, 1994: 11). By 2010, non-financial business owed US$1.3 trillion in bank loans, compared to US$4.6 in corporate bonds, a ratio of roughly 3.5:1 (Federal Reserve 2011: 66).

As would be expected, based on Zysman's work on the differences in financial organization across the globe, the proportions attributable to bank and non-bank sources of capital varied greatly depending on locality. Nevertheless, as early as 1992 an IMF-sponsored study noted that despite these 'pronounced differences ... the evidence indicates that the trend is toward a disintermediated, liquid, securitized structure' (Goldstein et al. 1992: 2–3). In Germany, for instance, International Monetary Fund figures indicate that in 1980 63 per cent of corporate borrowing was in the form of bank loans, while the comparable figures for Japan and the United States were 67 and 33 per cent respectively. By the turn of the millennium, bonds represented a significant funding source for non-financial business in both the United States and Japan; less so in the Eurozone but even here the prospects were positive as the introduction of the euro had spurred the corporate bond issuance of European companies (Hartmann et al. 2003: 10).

Why did disintermediation take off? A tentative answer revolves around the inherent costs of banking and the heightened competitive pressures of the world economy. Intermediation – in the sense of assuming the risk of defaulting loans – costs money. Banks have to establish and maintain infrastructures to check the creditworthiness of potential borrowers. They have to set the terms and conditions of loans, and administer and monitor them, which is unattractive to borrowers who want to manage their affairs. In cases of default, banks have to assume the burden of reducing their losses, which often involve them in expensive litigation (*The Economist* 1992: 9). Moreover, the environment in which banks have been doing business has changed in recent years, making this way of operating less attractive to depositors and borrowers. Because competitive pressures have been heightened by lower average growth and fewer barriers to trade, borrowers are more concerned with reducing their costs in whatever form, including the cost of capital. This cost-reduction impulse has been stimulated in borrowers just as the average cost of bank intermediated loans has risen due to the Basel capital adequacy standards which mandate banks to hold a certain ratio of reserve assets to loans outstanding. This is money that could otherwise be earning market-level returns. Lowell Bryan of the management consultancy McKinsey calculated the relative costs of bank intermediation versus securities financing. He found that the associated costs of lending money in the traditional way added over 200 basis points (hundredths of a per cent) to the total price of loans, whereas the total for securities financing was only around 50 points (*The Economist* 1994: 11). For a US$1 million loan, this makes a difference of US$15,000.

However, once more, states have been deeply implicated in the disintermediation trend. Regulative measures, such as the abolition of fixed commissions by the US Securities and Exchange Commission from 1972 onwards, and in the United Kingdom in 1986 as part of Thatcher's 'big bang' deregulation of financial markets, stimulated capital market growth. Moreover, states played more than a purely (de)regulatory role in getting these markets going. Often, their efforts have been constitutive for the emergence of these markets. This trend is particularly pronounced in East and Southeast Asia, where, in the wake of the Asian financial crisis of 1997–98, states have undertaken a number of individual and collective efforts to develop bond markets, such as the establishment of Asian bond funds to increase the

FIGURE 3.1A   Emerging Asia domestic financing patterns 2001

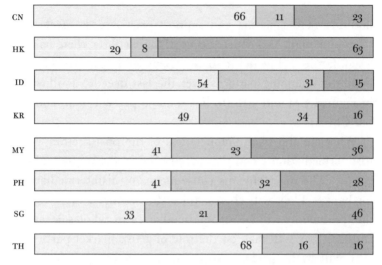

FIGURE 3.1B   Emerging Asia domestic financing patterns 2010

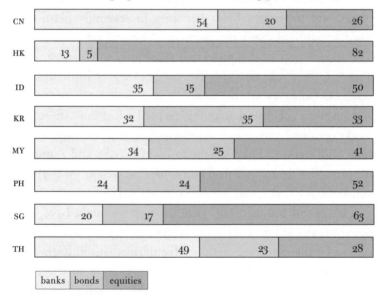

banks | bonds | equities

Key: CN People's Republic of China; HK Hong Kong; ID Indonesia; KR South Korea; MY Malaysia; PH Philippines; SG Singapore; TH Thailand.

Source: Asian Development Bank 2011, % of total domestic financing. The role of equity financing might be overstated as stock market capitalizations were taken as proxies for equities.

liquidity of the market and support price-finding mechanisms (Rethel 2010a). As a consequence of these efforts, there has been a significant decline in the share of bank lending as part of overall domestic financing patterns over the last decade, as illustrated in Figures 3.1a and 3.1b (to less than 50 percent in all countries but China).

What are the likely implications of the post-Bretton Woods disintermediation trend that accelerated in the 1990s and early 2000s? The most obvious consequence of disintermediation is for banks. They will change roles. Increasingly, they will give up the business of being intermediaries in wholesale capital. Instead, they will take on the role of active market participant: they will trade, package loans into securities, and devise new types of financial products. The distinction between commercial banks and brokerage firms becomes increasingly fictitious as commercial banks seek new sources of fee and arbitrage income. The significance of this process is that banks are being forced to abandon their role as authorities or gatekeepers in the financial markets. Contrary to the image of a dichotomy between state and market exchange, banks represented a fusion of these roles. Banks operated as hybrid institutions of collective action, between state and market. They sought to control risks and reduce the uncertainties for the political authorities, as well as for borrowers and lenders (Taylor and Singleton 1993: 204).

Things did not turn out quite the way we might have anticipated. Banks fought back hard against their potential marginalization by the emerging trend of disintermediation. Rather than settle for becoming irrelevant or minor players in the capital markets, the banks used their considerable capital bases and the lender-of-last-resort support they enjoyed from their governments and transformed themselves. The first decade of the twenty-first century bears witness to this shift. Banks became much bigger, often as a result of mergers. The decade from 1994 to 2003 saw more than 3,500 mergers in the United States alone, affecting institutions holding a total of assets worth more than US$3 trillion (Pilloff 2004). This included mergers between such renowned institutions as Chase Manhattan and JP Morgan in 2000, and the 1998 acquisition of BankAmerica Corp. by NationsBank that gave birth to the (at the time of writing) troubled Bank of America. Following the ultimate repeal of the Glass–Steagall Act in the USA in 1999, commercial banks moved into the markets with new speed, reflecting the removal of barriers between retail, commercial and investment banking activities. European banks also caught the capital markets bug and tried to strengthen the investment banking side of their business, for example by acquiring investment banking divisions, such as Deutsche Bank's acquisition of New York-based Bankers Trust Corporation in 1999 and/or by raising their profile in the City of London (see also Mügge 2010: 78–80). This pursuit of the disintermediation trend by European banks has to be understood against the backdrop of declining interest margins in Europe, falling from nearly 2.5 per cent in the mid-1980s to around 1.5 per cent in the mid-1990s (de Haan and Prast, as cited in Mügge 2010: 81).

Now many large European and American banks 'look much more like large highly-leveraged hedge funds' (Blundell-Wignall et al. 2009: 16). Much of the attraction lies in the potential for formerly rather staid institutions to engage in proprietary trading for the benefit of the bank, using the reserves of the bank and government support to underwrite the transformation. Banking has now, as Hardie and Howarth argue, become 'market-based banking' (2011: 2). At the same time as banks were fighting to transform themselves and avoid succumbing to disintermediation, the shadow banking system (non-depository institutions such as investment banks, hedge funds, money-market funds and insurers) grew greatly, so that by mid-2007 the assets of the shadow banks were larger than the total assets on bank balance sheets (Adrian and Shin 2010: 605). The point, following the line of Hardie and Howarth, is that depository banks have been playing the same game as the shadow banks, hedging the assets on their balance sheets just like these institutions (Hardie and Howarth 2011: 6). Interestingly, financial systems in many emerging market countries remain relatively dominated by traditional bank lending, suggesting much scope for the development of similar problems in these countries as their institutions flex their muscles and as governments seem to be keen to expand the role of capital markets (Thompson 2009: 209).

Extreme Financial Innovation and Uncertainty

It is in the context of the transformation of banks and the rise of the shadow banking system that we have to consider the astonishing financial engineering of the second half of the first decade of the twenty-first century. The subprime crisis that began in the summer of 2007 is one of the most traumatic global developments since World War II. Unlike wars and famine, this crisis and how it was caused caught the governing elites in rich countries unawares; it was something they had not wanted to see coming. The crisis and the deep recession it generated have caused dismay and at times panic as the depth of the problem revealed itself, especially in September 2008 with the bankruptcy of investment bank Lehman Brothers and the US$182 billion bailout of insurance giant American International Group (AIG).

The broad origins of the crisis can be found in the ending of the previous boom, with the bursting of the stock market mania for dotcom stocks in 2000. The US Federal Reserve responded to this market reversal with an easy money policy intended to make the cost of borrowing cheaper. The policy worked and interest rates fell. But the fall in rates had unanticipated effects. Looking for higher returns in a low-yield environment, banks sought out financial instruments that would deliver better profits. Structured finance had been around for several years but now it became the financial instrument of choice. Structured finance packages the debts most people incur – credit-card borrowings, car loans, mortgages – into securities that can be traded in financial markets. These securities gave their owners a claim on the revenues that those with the car loans, credit-card debt and mortgages provided. In a stroke a whole world of illiquid consumer debt was turned into financial market assets. Traders were then able to buy and sell these new bonds in the markets just as they traded the more traditional bonds issued by corporations, municipalities and national governments. At least for a time, financial alchemists had succeeded in their endeavour to turn base metal (subprime loans) or even air (synthetic credit products) into gold (AAA-rated certificates).

Securitization was big business. By 2006, the market had reached the size of an annual issuance of US$1.1 trillion, half of which were synthetic credit products (not backed by mortgages or any other real economy loans), pioneered by JP Morgan in 1997 (Blundell-Wignall 2007: 32; Johnson and Kwak 2010: 125). Moreover, whilst the size of these markets – an alphabet salad of ABS (asset-backed securities), MBS (mortgage-backed securities), CDOs (credit default obligations), CDO^2 (synthetic CDOs), CDS (credit default swaps) and so forth – at any given time was less than 1 per cent of world financial markets, their growth rates were the more astonishing. Many of the financial innovations that lay at their core only dated back to the 1990s or had until very recently played quite a marginal role. Yet the euphoria was not to last long and soon turned into the panic of 2007 and 2008.

The effects of securitization are pervasive. By selling on loans, banks can take them off their balance sheets and thus, it is thought, reduce their risk exposure. Moreover, by releasing capital, securitization also enhances liquidity. In theory, securitization aids the diversification of risk and could thus potentially lead to a more stable financial system (CGFS 2003). Yet in practice, due to the separation of originating and holding risk, securitization serves rather to increase risk (Best 2010; Langley 2008; De Goede 2004). The inherent uncertainty encountered in the pricing of these securities made the work of credit rating agencies the more important as they gave credibility and made it possible to assign a value to these structures (Langley 2008: 476–8). In other words, they played a constitutive role in making a market for structured debt securities possible.

The standard account of the subprime crisis reproduces the assumptions of the exogenous approach to financial crises discussed in Chapter 2. It is necessary, given this world-view, to find those institutions that did not do their jobs properly and make sure they do so in future. The crisis simply had to have external causes such as credit rating agencies or loans to low-income people. However, we suggest that the role played by these actors has to be understood differently, not as being external to the development of the market. Similarly, an interpretation that fits better is that the confidence in financial markets had, prior to 2007, became a mania, like so many before. Extreme financial innovation supported this mania, as cheap land development in Florida did during the 1920s. Given the dominance of exogenous views of the causes of financial crises, though, manias, panics and crashes are too often explained as the result of specific failures (such as the failure of credit rating agencies to value accurately the risk associated with structured finance) rather than understood as the result of social interactions at the height of a boom.

What Are Banks Today?

In the forty years or so between the end of the Bretton Woods system and today the standing of banks as social institutions has been transformed as the world they operate in has changed: their traditional cosy business model has been taken away by the rise of competitors such as the shadow banking sector premissed on financial disintermediation, and governments have pushed them to be more competitive. Banks have changed. They are much more aggressive institutions, aware of the risk of not meeting the competitive threat. Banks have as a result largely lost their diachronic role as social gatekeepers. Competition has taken power away from them, where power is understood as the ability of A to get B to do something B would otherwise not necessarily do (Lukes 1974). The banks' authority as institutions has been compromised.

Lincoln makes a key distinction between the epistemic authority of technical experts, scholars and professionals, who are 'an authority', and executive authority, of political leaders, military officers and police forces, those 'in authority' (Lincoln 1994: 3–4). What both have in common characterizes the *auctoritas* of Roman law, namely that they produce 'consequential speech' which quells doubts, winning the trust of audiences (Lincoln 1994: 4). Lincoln argues that the consequentiality of authoritative speech actually has little to do with the form or content of what is said. Instead, these consequences are best understood in 'relational terms as the effect of a posited, perceived, or institutionally ascribed asymmetry between speaker and audience'. This hierarchy allows some speakers, including banks and bankers, to command not just audience attention, but also their confidence, respect and trust (Lincoln 1994: 4). Lincoln concludes that historical circumstances are crucial to the existence of authority. Authority is best understood as an effect of these circumstances, rather than as an entity or a characteristic of an actor or institution. Its existence is therefore always contingent on time, place and circumstance. Capacities for producing these effects are central to understanding authority, as are understandings of who – what actors – has the capacity for producing the effect at specific times in particular places (Lincoln 1994: 10).

As Hannah Arendt observed, authority is defined in contra-distinction to both coercion by force and persuasion by argument (Arendt in Miller 1991: 29). Persuasion and coercion are implicit within authority, but are only actualized when authority itself is in jeopardy. Although implicitly constituting authority, their explicit actualization gives a signal that – at least temporarily – authority is negated (Lincoln 1994: 6). Epistemic authority is not imperme-able. Applying these claims to the circumstances of banking over the decades since the end of the Bretton Woods system suggests that the transformation of banking (and of financial markets gener-ally) has in most countries, including Germany and Japan, taken away any claim to authority on the part of banks. In this sense banking is greatly diminished as a social mechanism. Epistemic authority seems to be bivariate: authority either exists or is absent. Once generated, it is by its very nature hard to budge, as market participants tend to discount 'mistakes' or epistemic failures by authorities. But a fundamental change in the relationship between banks and their customers – a change in the structure of capital-ism – has removed epistemic authority from banks, and this has been reinforced by the global financial crisis.

Conclusion

Everybody is familiar with the rise of Internet book sales by Amazon and other companies since the mid-1990s. Bookselling used to be a comfortable business, but the rise of the online bookstore has greatly reduced margins as Internet sellers do not have to pay rents on fancy stores and so can undercut retail prices. This has led to the closure of many 'mom and pop' stores and compromised major book retailers too, as staff at Borders know to their cost. A similar process has been going on in global finance over the past few decades. When a company used to borrow from a bank it was in effect paying not just for the infrastructure of the bank but also for all the bad loans the bank had made to others. By deciding to seek funding in capital markets, borrowers could avoid these costs of intermediation and lower their costs of capital. In a world of increasing competition it is no surprise that wholesale bank lending has become more and more unattractive to borrowers and to the banks themselves. Banks have reacted to these latent trends by aggressively seeking to imitate the shadow banking system and have sought to make money in these markets by acting as agents to those seeking funding. Also, they have acted on their own behalf as market participants in what has come to be known as proprietary trading. Governments have been involved at every step, encouraging capital markets to expand sometimes in unregulated spheres, as in the case of the Euromarkets, and in accepting bank participation in these markets.

In this chapter we have argued that banks have undergone a major transformation over the past fifty years. Starting in the 1960s and accelerating with the end of the Bretton Woods system, banks have been under increasing pressure from the rise and rise of the capital markets and of the aggressive shadow banking institutions. Banks are no longer epistemic authorities. Their identity is no longer that of the wise judge, with a prudent eye, dubious of odd schemes of financial chicanery. Banks have pursued the yield curve vigorously in the most synchronic ways themselves, developing extreme forms of financial innovation, with calamitous consequences, as revealed by the global financial crisis. Moreover, the increasingly synchronic nature of banking operation has removed them further and further from the ideal-typical construct of the Jimmy Stewart banking model outlined in Chapter 1.

FOUR

SELF-REGULATION
AND RISK-TAKING

The developments we have discussed in financial markets contributed to change in the public regulation of banks. Financial innovation was accompanied by regulatory innovation as the rules for financial institutions changed quite substantially over the four decades before the global financial crisis erupted in 2007. More specifically, over the course of the 1980s and early 1990s, a convergence in regulatory thinking took place. This convergence was based on two principles. First, it was thought that the 'market would know best' when it came not only to the allocation of capital, but also to rewarding and disciplining the institutions and individuals involved in this endeavour. As a result, regulation focused on issues such as disclosure and transparency of operations to enable markets to play their disciplinary role better (see e.g. Best 2010; Palazzo and Rethel 2008).

Second, there was a sufficiently widespread consensus on the technical character of financial markets, subject to scientific explanation and manipulation (MacKenzie 2006). As a consequence, market actors, including banks, were thought to be rational processors of information. In the eyes of regulators and financial market practitioners alike, this made financial markets' calculable and excessive behaviour unlikely. In so doing, it made possible the reliance on regulatory devices such as the use of banks' own internal quantitative risk models and stress-testing conducted by banks within parameters chosen by themselves. Regulatory authorities played an increasingly hands-off role. As long as financial market regulators got the incentives right, market actors would adapt accordingly, leading to an efficient outcome. Or so it was thought.

This chapter discusses the impact of the trend towards self-regulation on the behaviour of banks. Governments changed their approach to banks between the end of the Bretton Woods system and the onset of the global financial crisis in 2007. They lost confidence in their ability to regulate banks and sought to push responsibility for prudent behaviour onto the institutions themselves. This move was underpinned by the perception that banks were too complex, acting in a context that was too rapidly evolving for any meaningful state regulation to be possible or affordable, given the high salaries in the financial sector, which made it difficult for the public sector to keep up. This further changed what banks did and the nature of banks themselves.

Whilst the pace, timing and intensity of this development differed across jurisdictions, it was nevertheless a global development in that regulators agreed that, for various reasons, regulation should be 'market enhancing' not 'market constraining' (see Mügge 2011: 190). As a consequence of this change in regulatory attitude, the ways banks operated became much riskier in the decades before the crisis erupted. And again it was public policy that shaped bank behaviour. More specifically, the push towards self-regulation on global and domestic levels, and – in the case of the EU – on the regional level, contributed to a very acute risk-taking culture. In so doing, policy further fostered a synchronic logic of bank operations and of financial markets more generally.

Moreover, remuneration became increasingly linked to the risk financial actors were thought to undertake and thus served as a further amplifier. According to an inquiry by the UK Treasury Select Committee, a booming bonus culture encouraged a proliferation of 'reckless and excessive risk-taking' by both individuals and institutions (Treasury Select Committee 2009: 3). This relationship is further elucidated by Marieke de Goede (2004: 207) who suggests that 'the financial speculator is valorised for willingly exposing himself to extreme and naturalised risk, which, if he operates wisely, holds out the promise of unprecedented profit.' Risk-taking, not the safe-keeping of deposits, for instance, became the new paradigm. Yet de Goede also cautions that 'this discourse obscures the aggregate risk of financial practices resulting from increased speculation, and the regressive distribution of wealth often associated with financial crises'.

To trace these developments, this chapter will look at moves towards bank self-regulation on a global level, more specifically the impact of the Basel Accord and its revisions, and at local and regional levels in the USA, East Asia and Europe. A result of the drive towards self-regulation was that banks tended to get bigger, as it was assumed that bigger banks would be more sophisticated and thus better able to regulate themselves, apart from profiting from economies of scale and scope. Again, this chapter supports our argument that public policy has been crucial in shaping banks. In so doing, it has played a fundamentally constitutive role which regulators nevertheless failed to embrace, or even to acknowledge.

The Move to Self-Regulation

Like banks themselves, bank regulators do not operate in a vacuum but are influenced by developments in their social and political environments. While the exact nature of bank regulation depends on the locality and time period under consideration, it is nevertheless possible to identify wider socio-political trends and principles that underpin attitudes towards banking regulation and that drive regulatory innovation. Indeed, the first chapter of this book identified two of these: the emergence of a new financial development paradigm that conceptualizes access to credit as a public good and the role of the international coordination of bank regulation in creating a level playing field for banks to compete on (see also Rethel 2010a; Foot and Walter 2010). The approach to financial regulation has changed considerably since the collapse of the original Bretton Woods system in the 1970s. Part of this was the changing material environment as reflected in increased financial disintermediation and the strategies of banks discussed in the previous chapter. It certainly heightened the pace of international financial markets and thus contributed to their increasingly synchronic logic (Yadav 2008: 12). However, the effect of changing ideas about how banks should be regulated and the role of the state in the economy more generally should not be ignored.

At the same time that financial disintermediation took off in the 1980s and 1990s, countries around the globe introduced a wide range of market-oriented regulatory reforms to their financial systems. The 1986 British 'big bang' and similarly dramatic changes in the regulation of the Japanese and US financial systems were perhaps the most noteworthy of these, given their importance as international financial centres. Steven K. Vogel (1996) has pointed out that the deregulation of financial markets was actually accompanied by a proliferation of new rules. Yet, importantly, in accord with the framework offered in this book, these rules were largely of a regulative nature and focused on constraining the conduct of financial actors, to a minimal degree. In accord with the exogenous view of crises, regulation became increasingly seen as external to market operations. Good regulation was understood not to interfere with the functioning of the market.

Despite the tendency in the literature to subsume all regulatory changes since the 1970s under the rubric of deregulation, it is clear that there was a marked shift from the deregulation approaches of the 1970s and 1980s to increased self-regulation in the 1990s and early 2000s. Whilst the first wave of deregulatory efforts changed the structure and intensity of regulation by creating a light touch, much less intrusive regulatory framework that would allow market forces to play freely (and profitably), the move towards self-regulation effectively changed the locus of regulatory authority, allowing financial institutions to set, enact and adjudicate their own rules of the game. It was based on faith in the self-correcting capacity of financial markets, in which the state only has to intervene in the (unlikely) case of market failure. Usually, it was thought, market discipline on its own would be sufficient to achieve efficient and stable outcomes. Public policy only had to create the conditions for market discipline to work. In this structurally deregulated framework, prudential regulation that focused on individual financial institutions was seen as sufficient to prevent excessive risk-taking by banks.

Nevertheless, there remained differences in the approach across jurisdictions. In the United States, belief in the self-correcting capacity of financial markets was perhaps the strongest. Not only were US markets the crucible of financial innovation, and US banks internationally leading in terms of market capitalization (for many an indicator of their financial might and sophistication), but policymakers – such as, most famously, the then chairman of the Federal Reserve Board, Alan Greenspan – were genuinely convinced of the optimality of self-regulation (Johnson and Kwak 2010). Whilst it is important to acknowledge that the strength of this belief varied across the plethora of US financial regulatory agencies (see Busch 2009: 49–54), it received further support from a series of academic impulses, most importantly the Efficient Market Hypothesis (discussed in Chapter 2), enhancing the credibility of this emerging world-view.

However, the move towards what effectively constituted a regulatory regime based on self-regulation was also closely linked to the lost confidence of regulatory agencies in their ability and capacity to regulate rapidly evolving financial markets. This was particularly acute with regard to the Basel capital adequacy regime. The provisions in the original Basel Accord issued in 1988 were deemed too crude, and as a consequence even technocrats themselves were 'not impressed by the ability of regulators … to design optimum rules for new and evolving financial markets' (David Mullins, cited in Yadav 2008: 9). Similarly, Rosemary Foot and Andrew Walter (2010: 234) suggest that '[r]egulators in the major international financial centres, particularly in New York and London, largely accepted this critique and argued that sophisticated banks should be permitted greater scope to manage their own risks.'

This trend was underpinned by the notion that regulation can only take place in hindsight and thus is not able to keep up with financial market developments. The alternative view, that public regulation should set the framework in which bank activity of all sorts takes place, was disregarded, if not altogether delegitimated by the belief in the efficiency of financial markets and the inefficiency of government intervention. In so doing, the move towards self-regulation also epitomized the near total acceptance of the synchrony of financial markets and the purely regulative character of financial regulation. By contesting the widely accepted instrumental and regulative character of regulation (e.g. expressed in Davies and Green 2010: 14) in favour of a constitutive understanding, we challenge this view in this book.

In much of Europe, the transition towards market self-regulation was slower to take off. This was due partially to the continued dispersal of regulatory authority within the European Union. Despite considerable achievements in creating a common market, member states retained domestic supervisory and regulatory structures vis-à-vis banks. Nevertheless, in terms of the principles underpinning financial regulation, a convergence on the premises of self-regulation can be identified over the course of the 1990s. For European policymakers, shifting towards self-regulation was a way to move beyond the national idiosyncrasies that continued to prevail with regard to the supervision and regulation of banks. This was closely linked to efforts to shift decision-making to the EU level (and away from national governments). As Mügge (2011: 196) suggests, '[i]n the face of rapid market transformation, so the argument went, the traditional co-decision procedure was too cumbersome for legislation to stay abreast of market developments.'

Once Europe had decided on financial market harmonization, and European banks such as ABN Amro, ING and Deutsche Bank played an important role in pushing for this, non-binding international norms were turned into European law (Mügge 2010: 56–8, 97). European policymakers implemented the 1988 Basel Accord, which was to be adopted on a voluntary basis and intended for internationally active banks only, in its 1989 Second Banking Coordination Directive. The 2004 Basel II Accord became enshrined in the 2006 Capital Requirements Directive. As a consequence, in Europe legislation actually played a much more significant role in strengthening the hold of the principle that 'the market knows best' than elsewhere. In so doing, the wriggle room for financial policymakers and regulators was increasingly narrowly circumscribed, whilst banks retained a certain freedom of interpretation with regard to their own risks.

Things were different in East Asia. In the decade before the outbreak of the global financial crisis, there was certainly not the same euphoria about unfettered markets as in the West. For Asian financial policymakers and business elites, the Asian financial crisis had seriously undermined faith in the self-correcting capacity of financial markets. As a consequence, policymakers remained much more pragmatic than their European and American counterparts. Mechanisms such as selective credit controls, capital controls and variable reserve requirements for banks firmly remained in the toolbox of financial regulators. Nevertheless, in the aftermath of the crisis, financial policymakers felt compelled to demonstrate increased efforts to 'upgrade' local financial systems, usually by implementing international (read Western) best practices. Moreover, particularly in South Korea, Thailand and Indonesia, the crisis led to a further opening up of domestic banking sectors to foreign participants whose operating principles sometimes differed quite significantly from those of indigenous financial institutions (Cook 2008). Malaysia, which, in responding to the Asian financial crisis, took a much more state-led approach than those other countries, increased its efforts to develop domestic capital markets and thus moved ahead with the disintermediation of its financial system (Rethel 2010b). Thus, financial norms in East Asia also underwent a series of transformations.

Like financial regulators elsewhere, Asian policymakers also focused on implementing market-enhancing policies, albeit for reasons different from their European and American counterparts and in different ways. In this case, the regulatory trends of the last decade have to be qualified as market development, not wholesale liberalization as in the West, as policymakers focused on putting into place what were deemed to be crucial market infrastructures. Nevertheless, given the damage that the Asian financial crisis had done to the (reputation of) local financial sectors, Asian policymakers were under pressure to demonstrate that they were implementing reforms that brought the region closer to international best practice. Basel II adoption was a means to showcase to the world the sophistication of local banks and their ability to compete internationally (Foot and Walter 2010).

The shift towards a rules-based system of prudential regulation, where regulators provide a detailed set of legalistic (or, in our framework, regulative) rules including specific measure of how they are to be implemented, was much more profound in the United States than the relatively more principles-based approach pursued by the Financial Services Authority in the United Kingdom, where regulators focused on providing a set of principles by which the industry was meant to abide. Nonetheless, it was in the nature of the European project to favour rules-based over principles-based approaches to regulation. In East Asia, moral suasion, heavily dependent on the status and charisma of regulators, continued to play an important role, albeit in combination with measures to make domestic banking sectors internationally more competitive and to build up capacity and regulatory expertise (Cook 2008; Hutchcroft 1998; Singh 1984). Whilst regulatory changes had the common purpose of enhancing markets, there were different pathways to achieving this outcome, via liberalization and self-regulation as in the US and European cases, or via market development as in the East Asian case. Nevertheless, in all three regions the balance of power shifted from regulators to market actors, although the extent to which this happened varied significantly.

The ideological shift towards self-regulation was accompanied by changes in the material capacity of states to regulate financial markets, especially so in the international financial centres. Core regulatory agencies in the major economies were seriously understaffed in the years that preceded the global financial crisis. For example, Tirole (2010: 26) claims that in the USA crucial work, such as investment bank solvency and liquidity, was regulated by the Securities and Exchange Commission with just seven people. In the UK, the main financial regulator, the Financial Services Authority, had pursued a policy of 'fewer, better staff'. As a result, and in combination with a high staff turnover, there was a lack of expertise in key areas such as prudential banking regulation, as the FSA's own (2008) investigation into the Northern Rock debacle suggests.

This picture reflects a wider trend with regard to the relationship between regulatory capacity and financial crisis. Grossman (2010: 270) suggests that a similar dynamic was at play in the run- up to the savings and loan crisis in the USA in the late 1980s. Here, a federal hiring freeze had led to a 20 per cent reduction in federal bank examinations, contributing to insufficient oversight. Whilst East Asian regulators largely seem to have defied this trend, this is likely a result of Asia's own crisis experience little more than a decade ago. Then, similar developments had taken place. For instance, only a few years before the 1997–98 financial crisis, Bank Negara Malaysia, the Malaysian central bank, had reduced staff levels by 50 per cent in core departments, including banking supervision (Government of Malaysia 1999: 26). This was widely seen as having contributed to its unpreparedness for the Asian financial crisis.

In addition to limits on and cuts in regulatory budgets, public pay scales in many countries made it impossible for financial regulators to match the salaries commanded in the financial sector. Thus, not only was the number of regulatory personnel in the advanced Western economies not on the same upward trajectory as that of people employed by the financial industry, but there was also an increased turnover in regulatory agencies as attractive financial sector compensation packages and career trajectories lured away staff. For many, working for a public regulator served as a stepping stone for getting a better paying job in the private financial sector. Thus, the median age of staff working in the UK Treasury is just a little over 30 (Macpherson 2011). Purely in terms of regulatory capacity, the regulated character of public-sector salaries proved disadvantageous in comparison to the self- (or market-) regulated nature of financial sector salaries. To give an example, in 2007 the permanent secretary of the UK Treasury, its highest ranked civil servant, received a salary in the region of £180,000, according to Treasury figures (HM Treasury 2008); Fred Goodwin, the now disgraced former CEO of Royal Bank of Scotland, earned £4.2 million in that year, including £2.86 million in bonuses (BBC News, 26 February 2009).

Compensation is another, often ignored, element of the self-regulation paradigm. Here again, as with the question of what constitutes legitimate bank activities and operations, financial market practitioners and most regulators agreed that decisions on compensation were best left to market forces, which had to compete internationally for the brightest and smartest. Furthermore, not just the size of compensation packages was left to the market, but also its composition. This resulted in the growing importance of supposedly performance-linked bonuses (exhibiting a marked upward bias). This further heightened the synchronicity and short-termism of financial markets (see also Harmes 1998).

It was not just public regulatory agencies that struggled to keep up with the salaries paid by the private sector. The trend also held true for what Jean Tirole (2010: 68) has called 'auxiliary regulators', namely the rating agencies. Here, the departure of staff 'lured by clients contributed to poor risk assessment' (Tirole 2010: 21). Regulatory changes in the decade before the global financial crisis did little to remedy this wider development. For example, in the United States the Sarbanes–Oxley Act of 2002 has been explicitly criticized for not addressing (the scandals') underlying causes, such as the short-term orientation of executive compensation (Suchan 2004: 25). Put briefly, compensation in the financial services industry provides another example par excellence of unfettered self-regulation gone awry.

The move towards self-regulating free markets was accompanied by the rhetoric that it would bring well-being and development to all. The global financial crisis has shown that this most certainly was not the case and that instead it created instabilities of a nearly unprecedented scale. However, financial industry self-regulation emerged as the dominant paradigm not only in the West but also became increasingly accepted in countries where the state had traditionally played a bigger role in the economy in recent decades. This only demonstrates the global dimension of the new paradigm, reinforced by regulatory changes, in particular the emerging Basel II consensus and associated changes in supervisory systems.

Self-Regulation:
Global and Domestic Interactions

If we look for crucial historical moments with regard to increased efforts to coordinate banking regulation based on prudential principles globally, then the international debt crisis of the 1980s and its aftermath have a strong claim (Kapstein 1992). Specifically where the international coordination of banking regulation is concerned, the origin is often dated back to the first Basel Capital Adequacy Accord (Basel I) of 1988. As we noted earlier, in the 1970s petroleum-exporting countries flush with oil money deposited their funds with Western banks and thus contributed to an international lending boom, fuelled by petrodollars. This was not sustainable and the system ultimately collapsed when Mexico had to call a moratorium on its debt in 1982, triggering what has become known as the international debt crisis, affecting the Latin American economies particularly badly. Nevertheless, it also strongly demonstrated the overexposure of Western (mainly, but not only, American) banks to Third World debt (Madrid 1992).

The international debt crisis had two important consequences for the further development of banking and its regulation. The conversion of international debt from bank loans to bonds that took place in the form of the so-called Brady Plan signalled an important move towards the disintermediation of emerging market debt. Moreover, the disintermediation of debt issued by emerging economics was mirrored by changes in the provision of credit, notably a marked shift within private-sector credit patterns from bank loans to portfolio investment. Thus the growth of financial disintermediation also has to be seen as an attempt to reduce the systemic threat posed by international bank loans, of which policymakers were made acutely aware during the 1980s by the international debt crisis (Rethel 2012). The global financial crisis that started in 2007 and a range of emerging market crises in the 1990s and early 2000s clearly demonstrate that this hope for greater financial stability because of increased financial disinter-mediation was not fulfilled.

The international debt crisis also gave momentum to efforts to coordinate the regulation of banks on a global level in the form of the first Basel Accord. In so doing, governments responded to the increasingly global nature of banking activity. Thus, Dewatripont et al. (2010: 2) suggest that the growing importance of large international banks raised expectations for states to create a level playing field for these institutions despite persistent variations in domestic regulation. Oatley and Nabors (1998) claim that the desire to redistribute the costs of regulation on a global level also played an important role in this regard. Nevertheless, Basel I signified a decisive shift towards regulating banks via prudential rules, most importantly those pertaining to minimum capital requirements. As Kapstein (1992: 267) points out, in the early 1980s the adoption of international rules pertaining to capital requirements was not a foregone conclusion. There was a range of other regulatory options that policymakers, at least theoretically, could have pursued. From the current vantage point, one such option that would have set the international financial system back on track, albeit coupled with a more intrusive approach to regulation, could have been debt forgiveness in combination with caps on future lending. Yet states chose to focus on prudential rules as the 'cornerstone of a new regulatory order' (Kapstein 1992: 283).

Prior to Basel I, progress had already been made on the international coordination of bank supervision. The collapse of the German Bankhaus Herstatt and the New York-based Franklin National Bank in 1974, in combination with the volatility of that time more generally, had drawn regulators' attention to the risks posed by internationally active banks and the uncertainties with regard to supervisory responsibilities. Therefore, in 1974 the Committee on Banking Regulations and Supervisory Practices was created. It was later renamed the Basel Committee on Banking Supervision (BCBS), the name under which it is known today. This grouping, originally consisting of the central bank governors of the Group of Ten countries, drafted an agreement in 1975, the so-called Basel Concordat, which set out some core responsibilities of home and host supervisors (Kapstein 1989). However, progress with regard to the international coordination of bank regulation would have to wait another decade.

Following the turmoil of the 1980s, in early 1987 the US Federal Reserve Board and the Bank of England announced that they had agreed on a common standard for bank capital adequacy rules. After nearly a year of intense negotiations, the Basel Committee announced in December 1987 that its members had agreed on a common capital standard, which would become known as the Basel Accord. It set out minimum capital adequacy requirements for internationally active banks with an overall capital ratio of 8 per cent. Important elements of the definition of capital and the assessment of risk remained within the remit of regulatory control. The Accord offered only a very limited range of what were increasingly deemed to be very crude risk weightings. Over the course of the 1990s this was undermined by an international bank lobby which argued that the original Basel Accord was insensitive to the actual risk exposure of financial institutions, and thus advocated a more nuanced approach to risk weightings. For this purpose, they favoured the use of bank internal risk-assessment models. And financial regulators concurred with their view.

The strongest push towards bank self-regulation of risk on the global level yet was made with the introduction of the Basel II framework. The original Basel Agreement focused on credit risk. However, in the 1996 Market Risk Amendment it was extended to cover market risk. This was closely linked to the approval of risk models applied by banks internally to measure the risk exposure of their portfolios. Thus, the push towards greater self-regulation gained momentum in the mid-1990s. It was also meant to address the growing importance of disintermediated financial markets. As Davies and Green (2010: 39) suggest, 'much of the preparatory work for the market risk package was undertaken jointly with securities supervisors with the intention that the methodology could also be used for non-bank financial institutions and particularly for the large security houses.' Boundaries between the different segments of financial markets and their regulation had become increasingly porous.

Nevertheless, the changes introduced with the Market Risk Amendment were still not deemed enough to address the growing complexity of financial markets and what was perceived to be the costly burden of the rather unspecific Basel I regulations. This thinking, coupled with intense lobbying by big banks, culminated in the successful completion of the Basel II Accord in 2004 (Davies and Green 2010: 39–44). The core elements of Basel II consisted of: (1) risk-weighted minimum capital requirements; (2) periodic supervisory review; and (3) market discipline. It covered credit risk, market risk and operational risk (De Goede 2004: 209). However, where Basel II substantially departed from the previous arrangements is in the use of internal (a bank's own) risk assessment in determining the capital to be held by the bank. There was also greater reliance on self-regulation and market mechanisms with regard to the role envisaged for credit rating agencies in the Basel II framework. Its emphasis on market discipline further enshrined the 'the market knows best' principle.

Value-at-risk (VaR) modelling, pioneered by US investment banks such as Bankers Trust and JP Morgan, calculates daily risk exposures based on historical values. Since its origins in the late 1980s and early 1990s, this market invention has turned into a market convention and is used every day in most banks, although there are also other models such as risk-adjusted return on capital (RAROC) (Power 2005). The use of VaR has been criticized from the outset for relying too much on (historical) quantitative data and in so doing giving market participants a false sense of security (Taleb 2010). Indeed, it is based on the same linear axiom as the EMH. Nevertheless, and this is the crux, the adoption of such models in the 1996 Market Risk Amendment to the original Basel Accord and in Basel II put this contested method at the forefront of (self-)regulatory efforts. As De Goede (2004: 210) argues,

> The assumption that VaR reflects unproblematically real world possibilities enabled it to become the basis of extreme financial risk-taking and profit-making without a semblance of security. ... By accepting VaR – and similar – risk measures as the basis for

capital requirements, the BCBS legitimates and gives authority to these contested risk models.

One of the problems with the approach of the new Basel II regime was that it created even greater incentives for financial institutions to move liabilities off their balance sheets to reduce the amount of capital they would have to hold in reserve and thus their costs. This contributed to the growth of a shadow banking system consisting of special purpose vehicles (SPVs) and other non-deposit-taking entities. In this regard, banks operated as important conduits channelling money into the shadow banking system, by selling on loans they had originated. Yet, as Kapstein (1989: 325) pointed out more than two decades ago for the case of the United States, '[o]ne of the foundations of the American financial system is that banks act as impartial analysts of credit risk. Can this role be maintained when banks simply originate transactions that are subsequently repackaged and sold to investors?' The answer, as became very clear during the run-up to and subsequent unfolding of the global financial crisis, was that it could not. Instead of keeping risky mortgages, especially in the subprime segment, on their books, these were repackaged as securities and sold on. The idea was that in such a system risk would be borne by those with the highest capacity to do so, for a reward. Indeed, Basel II created perverse incentives: as banks were becoming more and more obsessed with the risk exposure of their own books, they were less and less concerned with the creditworthiness of the borrowers to which they lent. This made a joke out of the idea of market discipline, where banks reward creditworthy borrowers with loans and deny the profligate credit. Instead, it contributed to the growing misallocation of credit (Johnson and Kwak 2010: 147).

There were some warning signals as to the soundness of such thinking. For example, in 2003 the Basel-based Committee on the

Global Financial System set out the potential dangers associated with credit risk transfer (CGFS 2003). However, these more cautious voices were generally ignored in the euphoria of the mid-2000s. Moreover, a later report, commissioned by the Basel-based Financial Stability Forum, concluded that the benefits of the newly emerging instruments to transfer credit risk outweighed the problems. As we know, the system did not work out as its advocates had hoped. Risk ended up where it should not be (i.e. with risk-averse investors such as pension funds and city councils) and, instead of being dispersed throughout the system and thus diversified away, there remained lumps of high risk concentration. Banks were more exposed than they had thought. Thus, risk transfer certainly did not live up to the expectations placed upon it.

As became very apparent during the global financial crisis that started in 2007, self-regulation, based on the notion that markets were best left to policing themselves and would achieve a stable and efficient outcome on their own, in combination with a 'scientific' understanding of risk, was highly problematic. It pushed banks further down a trajectory of increasingly synchronic bank operations. Yet, while the move towards self-regulation as a *public policy* has received some attention in the literature, its importance for the behaviour of banks has been underappreciated. The next section turns to the relationship between a regulatory framework based on self-regulation and the risk-taking behaviour of banks and bankers.

The Self-Regulation Risk-Taking Nexus

Banks have always wanted to make a profit, and there is little to suggest that either the developments of the 1980s and the 1990s or the global financial crisis have had any fundamental impact on this motive. However, what changed in the run-up to the recent global financial crisis was that profit-making was increasingly equated with risk-taking. This is actually a fundamental reconfiguration of banking's legitimate objectives, a key constitutive rule change. The deregulation of interest rates in the 1970s and 1980s, in combination with the move to floating exchange rates, the introduction of the euro in Europe and the disintermediation of financial markets, put severe pressure on the traditional revenue models of banks (see also Ertürk and Solari 2007). Financial institutions (and their employees) now had to become risk-takers and, in their view, taking these risks warranted their high compensation packages. Underlying this transformation was the notion that a bank's risk was both quantifiable and calculable and as a consequence that it could be fully understood and scientifically explained. And this was big business. As de Goede (2004: 197) suggests, '[t]he identification, calculation, pricing and packaging of risk are at the heart of the rapid expansion of modern financial markets on a global scale.' In addition, banks' claims that they could meaningfully assess the credit risk to which they were exposed, and about 'their own incentives and capacity to manage exposures', were taken at face value (Mügge 2011: 199). In so doing, a direct link between risk and reward could be established, contributing to the emergence and proliferation of a 'risk-taking culture'.

The irony, of course, is that despite all this hype about banks and bankers as risk-takers, what they effectively did was to speculate with 'other people's money' without having to assume full liability for their actions. Unlike in other 'risk-taking' professions such as coal mining or soldiering, the actual risks to which bankers were personally exposed were limited. All they could lose was their reputation, a weak threat following the successful reinvention of Michael Milken as philanthropist and the rather muted reactions to the analyst scandals of the early 2000s. They might not get their bonuses, which despite lacklustre performance in the bear market of the first decade of the twenty-first century continued on an upwards trend; or, in the worst case, they could lose their job. There was little threat to the life and physical 'integrity' of bankers, at a time when battle deaths in the Iraq and Afghanistan wars reached new heights for both the USA and the UK. Instead of actual risk-taking, what banks and bankers learnt to excel at was *rent extracting*. In turn, the risk-taking culture, in all its institutional and individual dimensions, heightened the synchronicity of bank operations and engendered for itself wider public acceptance. Important here is to note the twofold impact of the self-regulation paradigm: it penetrated financial markets not just in terms of risk assessments and the way that risk exposures were managed, but also in terms of executive compensation. In so doing, a financial bomb with a short fuse was created. In this context, the crisis in the subprime loan market was just a spark that set the whole construction alight, following closely on a decade that had witnessed the increasing conflation of risk and profit. Because profitable risk was taken by bankers with other people's money, rapidly rising leverage ensued.

Regulators and financial market practitioners shared a very similar notion of risk. By endorsing a 'scientific' understanding of risk, regulation again played a constitutive role, instead of a merely regulative/constraining one, but it did so largely unconsciously. The transformation of banks from market authorities to market participants was rooted in this reconceptualization of risk, the purpose of bank operations and the unconstrained pursuit of profit. This was compounded by the link between risk-taking and remuneration that was entrenched in the minds of both market practitioners and policymakers. The inauspicious dynamics this created were exacerbated by high liquidity in an ignored but nevertheless acutely inflationary environment which further cancelled out market discipline. Where market discipline failed – and this was apparent even before the bubble burst and the crisis ultimately erupted – there would have been even greater need for regulators to play their role. Despite the regulatory changes of the 1990s and 2000s, this was still a distinct possibility. As Thirkell-White (2009: 710) points out, '[f]ailures in national regulation were partly influenced by international trends and financial sector pressure for equal treatment. However, there was little in the global regime actually to stop regulators from doing their jobs.' Yet they did not do their jobs as they should have.

The impact of what Jean Tirole (2010: 12) identifies as 'inappropriate and poorly implemented regulation' in the run-up to the crisis was heightened as global regulation is implemented, monitored and enforced by national regulatory agencies. In so doing, financial regulators act as a link between the domestic and the global levels. In this regard, the anticipation of the new Basel II arrangements played a significant role as financial institutions began to adapt their behaviour and so did regulators. The changes caused by the domestic preparation for the implementation of Basel II had profound implications across different jurisdictions. More particularly, it created regulatory risk in that it tied up resources and ultimately hampered the effectiveness of day-to-day regulation. For example, the UK Treasury Select Committee (2008) report on the run on Northern Rock and the FSA's own investigation (2008) make for chilling reading, given the number of regulatory mistakes they identify. Yet these mistakes were compounded by efforts to anticipate the implementation of the Basel II regime. Not only did they lead to an increased workload for the regulatory agencies, in particular the Financial Services Authority, tasked with the supervision of banks. It also changed the way that banks were regulated. Thus, Northern Rock was granted a 'Basel II waiver' in that it was allowed to rely more on its own estimates of its risk exposure. That this was not a purely numerical and technical change is indicated by the fact that, because of this waiver, Northern Rock announced an increase in its dividend in July 2007, less than two months before the bank run occurred. It cited improved risk weightings and, based on this, a reduction of capital requirements as the reason for the dividend increase (Treasury Select Committee 2008: 25). To keep a long story short, as regulatory institutions focused on the changes brought about by the implementation of Basel II, they neglected their day-to-day regulatory activity.

What was similarly remarkable in the run-up to the global financial crisis that started in 2007 was the extent to which financial regulators had divested themselves of regulatory tools such as selective credit controls, especially in the West. Constraints on regulators were exacerbated in Europe because of the rule of home regulation (Rosenbluth and Schaap 2003: 335). The failure to embrace and instead effectively ignore the constitutive character of regulation further drove risk-taking. Nevertheless, the move to Basel II also contributed to risky behaviour in less obvious ways. It pushed the idea that the bigger a bank was, the better equipped it would be to self-regulate itself to the limits. This created incentives for banks to expand rapidly. In so doing, the capacity to self-regulate was not merely seen as the product of bank sophistication but conversely bank size acted as a signal of a bank's sophistication and international competitiveness. Thus, for example, between 1990 and 2008 the share of financial assets held by America's ten biggest banks quintupled from 10 per cent to 50 per cent (Ferguson 2009). There was too little consideration of the more significant systemic risk that bigger banks (and their collapse) posed or their growing capacity to extract rents. Moreover, there were similarly misaligned incentives for financial regulators to push their banks to adopt internal ratings-based

(IRB) approaches. As Davies and Green (2010: 45) lament, '[u]nfortunately, as these ... approaches are seen as indicators of sophistication, some countries whose banks are ill-suited to Advanced IRB are mandating its adoption.'

Similar developments can also be identified in East Asia, despite the qualification in terms of the adoption of the 'market knows best' principle outlined above. In Malaysia during the run-up to the Asian financial crisis of 1997–98 a comparable view with regard to the relationship between less intrusive regulation and bank size had taken hold. It was based on the notion that the bigger the balance sheet, the more sophisticated banks would be, requiring less oversight. This was closely linked to the implementation of Basel I at the time. The Malaysian central bank introduced a two-tier regulatory system where tier one banks (the tiering among other things being determined by value of capital) were given greater flexibility with regard to their banking operations (Government of Malaysia 1999: 25). This contributed to the rapid and reckless expansion of loan books. Indeed, at the time of writing, some of the biggest banks by market capitalization are located in East Asia, more specifically China. The notion that bigger banks have more sophisticated ways of dealing with risk is false and turns banks into beasts that are even harder to tame.

The moves towards self-regulation and increased risk-taking by both individual bankers and financial institutions more generally were closely intertwined. Based on the notion that risk could be scientifically identified and quantified, and that banks themselves were best positioned to assess their exposure to risk, financial regulators neglected their basic duties. Bonus-linked financial compensation packages amplified the risk that bankers were willing to undertake. However, this system of credit risk transfer only worked as long as markets were going up and as long as investors were prepared to continue to purchase risky assets. When market sentiment faltered, the whole pyramid collapsed.

Conclusion

In recent decades, global and domestic regulatory efforts became increasingly focused on designing regulative rules of conduct for banks. The move towards increased self-regulation by banks was a core element in this regard. Not only were banks more or less allowed to decide themselves on the scope of their operations and the risk they wanted to take, but they also could design their own compensation packages. This was to the neglect of explicit constitutive rules that could have set the basic framework in which banks were to operate and heightened the synchronicity of bank operations. Whilst banking was transformed rapidly, this transformation lacked a coherent legitimacy that could have been derived from a societal consensus on what the role of banks – and finance more generally – was to be. Through self-regulation, banks became more and more disembedded from society and operated increasingly outside any meaningful societal or political control. Nevertheless, the global financial crisis that began in 2007 should have brought home the fallacy of assuming a separate financial–economic sphere that would control itself via market discipline.

In hindsight, the trend towards self-regulation exacerbated both the increasingly synchronic logic of banks and financial market operations and the understanding of regulation as being primarily tasked with creating rules of conduct, not purpose, for banks. Policymakers seriously underestimated the extent to which these regulatory changes would shape the way that banks operated. In terms of the analytical scheme developed in Chapter 1, it pushed bank operations further towards the third quadrant in Figure 1.1 and away from the economically and socially better adjusted first quadrant of a reflexive banking model. The global financial crisis has significantly undermined both the intellectual and the practical foundations of the principle that 'the market knows best'. It has demonstrated that financial markets are social constructs, that financial market actors can act irrationally within certain group settings, and that scientific explanations of markets and behaviour have serious shortcomings vis-à-vis sociological ones. So a regulative understanding of financial regulation has to be severely criticized. Yet, have the right lessons been learnt? And, perhaps even more importantly, have they led to the right policy recommendations? In the next chapter, we will critically evaluate a range of reform proposals that have been put forward by various regulators, academics and financial market practitioners.

FIVE

PROBLEMS WITH
REFORM PROPOSALS

In many cases, the short-term response to the problems that banks experienced at the height of the recent financial crisis was to re-capitalize them with public funds. In some cases, this culminated in the wholesale nationalization of a number of what were thought to be systemically significant banks. However, not only was 'bank nationalisation ... a policy reversal that delivered more of the same' (Froud et al. 2010: 32) in that it did not mean a renunciation of the dominant market paradigm, but it was also always meant as only a temporary measure. As governments around the globe have again started to divest themselves of their shares in banks obtained during the crisis, numerous reform proposals have been mooted in both domestic and international financial policymaking circles. Perhaps ironically, what seems to have emerged as the common denominator of these reform proposals is that they are intended to make future interventions by the state in the financial system less likely. That is, current reform proposals do not challenge the prevailing 'the market knows best' paradigm.

Some of these reform proposals – for example, with regard to the standardization of financial products and the movement of these products onto exchanges as well as the more direct and

intrusive regulation of hedge funds – acknowledge, at least implicitly, the growing complexity of international financial markets and
the increasingly arbitrary distinction between banks and so-called
non-bank financial institutions (see Hardie and Howarth 2011).
Others, such as the revision of the Basel framework (Basel III),
focus on the coordination of international regulatory efforts,
despite recent calls for paying more attention to strengthening domestic regulatory capacities and frameworks (see e.g. Thompson
2010; Rodrik 2009). Nevertheless, most of these proposals bear
testimony to the fallacious thinking that we can prevent future
banking crises by regulating against a repeat of the most recent
crisis. Much the same thing happens in the fight against terrorism
in commercial aviation as new technologies such as shoe scanners
are introduced in response to new experiences.

This tendency is exacerbated by the fact that those financial
market and policy elites most profoundly implicated in the emergence of the recent financial crisis are again walking the corridors
of power with renewed confidence and remain key actors (agenda-
setters and decision-makers) when it comes to financial reform.
This includes market practitioners and their associations, such
as the Institute of International Finance, a grouping of more than
450 internationally active financial institutions that has actively
sought to influence the regulatory response in the wake of the
global financial crisis. It also pertains to public regulators and
policymakers, both on the national level and internationally;
take, for example, the Basel Committee on Banking Supervision
currently in the process of rewriting the Basel rules. This has
implications for the range and type of reform proposals thought
to be conceivable. As Anna Leander convincingly argues,

> The close range of the financial reform process is intrinsically tied
> to its anchoring in reformers' shared understanding of financial
> markets; a doxa [a common belief or mental framework] that

shapes the regulatory discussion among financial regulators. Although there is plenty of room for critique and even if the doxa may evolve in time, it limits the reform discussions and the understanding of the politics involved. It casts options that fall outside a relative restricted area as unprofessional and unserious. (Leander 2009: 465)

So how do we situate current reform proposals in our scheme? With regard to the question of the constitutive or regulative nature of newly emerging regulatory rules, we can distinguish between proposals that fall in the category of structural regulation (e.g. pertaining to market entry; separation of or restrictions on certain activities) and those that refer to prudential regulation (e.g. with regard to capital adequacy rules and reserve ratios). Structural regulation is more likely to embrace the constitutive aspect of regulation and its impact on bank behaviour, whilst prudential regulation continues to be very much focused on designing rules for the conduct of banks.

Another way to demarcate different regulatory approaches is to distinguish between rules-based and principles-based regulation, with the former often thought to reflect the US approach to financial market regulation and the latter that of the UK. However, again we see that the speed of convergence has picked up in the aftermath of the financial crisis. Effectively, the crisis has reinforced the shift towards more rules-based regulation, even though rules-based regulation worked no better than principles-based regulation. As a consequence, the intent of regulation has become even more deeply regulative than constitutive in nature (and further entrenches the shift towards a US-style system of rules-based financial regulation). This has been exacerbated by post-crisis reform proposals: take, for example, the new UK Prudential Regulatory Authority's (PRA) focus on 'managing rather than preventing failure' and establishing rules in this regard that has been touted as a 'big change in prudential regulation' (*Financial Times*, 13 December 2010).

Where does this leave us with regard to the synchronic or diachronic nature of banking operations? One of the major criticisms of the period in the run-up to the recent financial crisis was that bank regulation had become more and more procyclical, compounding the increasingly synchronic way that banks behaved/invested. In that some of the reform proposals, in particular those pertaining to macroprudential policies, call for a more countercyclical approach, at least with regard to capital adequacy requirements, this position seems to have slightly shifted. Nevertheless, as macroprudential policies still focus very much on the time span of short- and mid-term business cycles, we think they still do not go anywhere far enough in terms of instilling a more diachronic investment culture, as we discuss in more detail below. In other words, and to paraphrase Froud et al., not only the immediate response to the crisis but also longer-term efforts at introducing new banking regulation have effectively amounted to more of the same.

To substantiate this point, this chapter examines in more detail a range of proposals that have been put forward to reform banking regulation. Our view on these proposals is very clear: we do not think that these reforms adequately address the problem with banks. More specifically, we will look at three issue areas: macroprudential policies (including some of the new Basel III specifications), the banning of proprietary trading (the so-called Volcker rule), and seemingly more radical proposals to break up the banks to achieve a more competitive market structure, as recently put forward, for example, in Britain. We suggest that these proposals ignore the constitutive role played by government when it comes to shaping the nature of banks. Similarly, they fail to counteract, or in some cases even address, the increasingly

FIGURE 5.1   Reform proposals in perspective

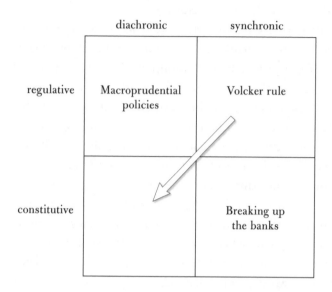

synchronic nature of banking practice. Thus, just breaking up banks, applying the Volcker rule or creating mechanisms for improved macroprudential regulation are in our view not sufficient to come to terms with the problem with banks. This is also highlighted by looking at Figure 5.1, which portrays where these three sets of reform proposals have to be situated in our analytical scheme.

Current reform proposals are hardly the decisive shift away from the pre-crisis doxa, which is how they are often presented, and that is indicated by the arrow in Figure 5.1. Indeed, it is questionable whether the problem with banks can ever be fully solved and whether we could move to reflexive banking, especially within the current mindset. Moreover, if the recent financial crisis has taught us a lesson, then it is the problematic nature of one-size-fits-all regulatory measures. Yet this is something that most of these reform proposals fail to address.

The Problem with Banning Proprietary Trading

The policy of banning proprietary trading has received the most support in the United States. Named after former chairman of the Federal Reserve Board, Paul Volcker, the Volcker rule is often portrayed as a decisive move against the speculative behaviour of banks, as it is intended to prevent them from trading on their own books. In January 2010 President Barack Obama endorsed the proposals made by Paul Volcker (White House 2010). Subsequently, the Volcker rule was enacted as a late addition to the Dodd–Frank Wall Street Reform and Consumer Protection Act that passed Congress in the summer of 2010. President Obama observed, with the Volcker rule '[b]anks will no longer be allowed to own, invest or sponsor hedge funds, private equity funds or proprietary trading operations for their own profit' (White House 2010). For this purpose, the rule prescribes a cap of 3 per cent on how much bank tier 1 capital (i.e. core capital) can be invested in hedge and private equity funds and how much of such a fund can be owned by an individual bank.

Advocates of a ban on proprietary trading have suggested it would limit the risks financial firms take (White House 2010). As Obama put it,

> we should no longer allow banks to stray too far from their central mission of serving their customers. In recent years, too many financial firms have put taxpayer money at risk by operating hedge funds and private equity funds and making riskier investments to reap a quick reward. And these firms have taken these risks while benefiting from special financial privileges [i.e. potential access to government bail-out funds, thus reducing their financing costs] that are reserved only for banks. (White House 2010)

Whilst this move is seemingly targeted at future behaviour and is not supposed to be regulation in hindsight, it effectively responds to the behaviour of investment banks, such as New

York-based Goldman Sachs, in the run-up to and during the recent financial crisis (Volcker 2010). Indeed, if there is one institution that has drawn criticism like no other in the wake of the crisis, it is Goldman Sachs. Not only were its close political connections perceived as a massive asset when it came to its being spared the worst effects of the crisis, but Goldman Sachs then actually also used the crisis as a crucial opportunity to make profit, resulting in a 48 per cent increase in staff compensation for 2009 (BBC News, 21 January 2010; Johnson and Kwak 2010; Johnson 2009). This was after Goldman Sachs had accepted US$10 billion as part of the Troubled Assets Relief Programme, the US government bail-out fund, which has since then been fully repaid.

Goldman Sachs has epitomized for many the degree of regulatory capture in the US financial system in the run-up to the recent financial crisis (Johnson 2009). Over the decades, a number of former Goldman Sachs bankers had moved on to become US Treasury Secretaries in both Democrat and Republican administrations (see e.g. Paulson 2010; Rubin and Weisberg 2003). When appointed they took former Goldman Sachs employees with them to staff some of the most important US financial regulatory agencies. Ever since the most recent crisis broke, Goldman Sachs has been beset by a series of scandals that put into question its ability to manage conflicts of interest successfully. These included a complaint by the US Securities and Exchange Commission (SEC) about Goldman Sachs mis-marketing some of its structured products (ABACUS 2007–AC1 to be precise) by not disclosing that Goldman's had actually allowed the counterparty (the hedge fund Paulson & Co.) to pick the underlying assets.

Goldman Sachs was not alone in creating and mismanaging conflicts of interest and giving room to scandalous behaviour with regard to its proprietary trading activities. Moreover, perhaps it is a little unfair to single out Goldman Sachs in this regard as its risk management systems have, at least so far, prevented the more self-destructive potential of proprietary trading. A drastic example where proprietary trading ultimately resulted in the demise of the financial institution itself was provided in the mid-1990s by the long-established British investment house Barings. Here, the speculations of a Singapore-based employee, Nick Leeson, caused losses of up to £1 billion, which the institution was unable to absorb. Ten years after the Barings crisis, this type of situation had become even more problematic, exacerbated by the explosive combination of proprietary trading with high levels of leverage. Thus, in 2008 the French bank Société Générale suffered losses of US$6.7 billion, again from proprietary trading activities gone awry. The individual, Jérôme Kerviel, was found guilty of fraud in October 2010 and sentenced to five years in prison. And banks do not seem to have learnt their lessons from the crisis, as internal risk management systems continue to fail to prevent this sort of activity. In September 2011 Swiss bank UBS revealed that a trader in its London office had lost US$2.3 billion in unauthorized trades (Carter and Protess 2011).

Proprietary trading has been a recurrent challenge to the smooth operation of financial markets. These and similar actions contributed to heightened volatility in international financial markets and gave way to a sharp sense of financial instability and vulnerability. Nevertheless, whilst the financial institutions concerned were quick in singling out the fraudulent behaviour of individuals and thus tried to externalize the blame, the frequency of these occurrences suggests they are a more systemic feature than often is acknowledged. In other words, the incentives that proprietary trading creates foster a culture of gambling and are largely institutional and not just personal or individual in nature (see Palazzo and Rethel 2008).

In practice, the rules designed with regard to proprietary trading are not primarily intended to prevent excessive proprietary trading and risk-taking as such, with the closely associated impact on the stability of the financial system, but to prevent the state from having to bail out those institutions involved. Thus, it is important to note that not all financial firms are banned from proprietary trading. The rule is not a blanket ban on the range of speculative behaviour by banks that gave cause to so much distress and hardship in the global financial crisis. The ban on proprietary trading applies only to deposit-taking institutions. It will make it more difficult for them to serve as a conduit to the shadow-banking system. Credibility issues aside, it is questionable whether the Volcker rule is an appropriate response given the proliferation of non-traditional banking activities that make the old distinction between investment banking and commercial banking increasingly untenable. In so doing, however, its potential effects on shadow banking are not clear. Often the line between client-oriented activities such as market-making (i.e. providing liquidity to a market by being able to buy and sell an asset independent of there being a customer order or not, which could potentially lead to building up an inventory in this asset) and proprietary trading is blurred (Carter and Protess 2011).

Moreover, financial institutions can choose whether they want to be deposit-taking banks or not and thus if they would fall within the remit of the Volcker rule. This ambiguity about whom the rule will apply to, given the voluntary basis of bank designation, has led to a range of criticisms. Indeed, similar to the 'choose your own regulator' approach discussed in Chapter 1, financial institutions can decide whether they would prefer to operate in an environment with weaker regulation, by forfeiting the right to take in deposits. This regulatory framework will certainly continue to foster a culture of regulatory arbitrage. In so doing, banning proprietary trading on its own does not address one of the root causes of the recent financial crisis, namely the degree of leverage in the international financial system, made possible among other things by implicit state bail-out guarantees. Most importantly, it has been alleged that financial institutions other than deposit-taking banks, which will continue to conduct proprietary trading activities, would in the event of another crisis still seek the protection of the safety net provided by the state. After all, would the government really refuse to bail out institutions whose collapse could entail a systemic meltdown?

Another major drawback of the Volcker rule is that it is specifically designed for the US financial system and little effort has been put into rolling it out more widely. The fact that the rule will apply only to US financial institutions and those that operate in the USA makes it questionable if, for example, the recent UBS scandal would have been within its remit. In the UK, the governor of the Bank of England, Mervyn King, has voiced these concerns. Currently, the Volcker rule's implementation creates an 'unlevel' playing field to the advantage of East Asian and European banking sectors. It creates even stronger incentives for regulatory arbitrage both within the United States and across jurisdictions. In so doing, it does not constitute an effective response to the structural causes of the crisis, but is 'more of the same'.

Thus, when it comes to evaluating the Volcker rule critically, not just as a means to regulate proprietary trading but to reduce risky behaviour by banks more generally, it scores very low. It is a rule of conduct rather than a rule of purpose, limiting the scope of certain activities of deposit-taking banks but not reshaping their identities. It neither addresses the increasingly synchronic nature of banking operations nor embraces the constitutive character of financial regulation. The only change is that deposit-taking institutions are not allowed to speculate on their own books.

Indeed, we think that policymakers have been conspicuously silent about future risk-taking activities by banks to which it might give cause. It does not take leverage out of the system. Similarly, it is questionable whether the rule will truly be binding. As a consequence, uncertainty persists about whether the problem of moral hazard – for example, the greater risk taken by these institutions as they rely on the implicit protection and potential bail out by the state and taxpayer – would really be sufficiently addressed. Nevertheless, perhaps it is worthwhile remembering Leander's claim. After all, the Volcker rule is named after one of the most eminent financial policymakers, not just in the USA but globally. This is clearly highlighted by Paul Volcker's membership in the Group of Thirty, the international body of leading financiers and academics (Tsingou 2007). This proposal certainly falls within a narrowly circumscribed area of what types of reform are deemed not just desirable but, even more fundamentally, possible. As a weak reincarnation of the 1933 Banking Act, it certainly does not herald the progressive change in how states approach banks that is warranted.

The Problem with Breaking Up the Banks

As with the ban on proprietary trading, several rationales have been put forward to support the idea of breaking up the banks. They include the greater risk posed by systemically important financial institutions and the burden that having to bail out these institutions presents for taxpayers; competition issues affecting the orderly and cost-efficient provision of financial services; and the desired risk exposure of ordinary bank deposits. With regard to the first issue, the notion that in the run-up to the global financial crisis that began in 2007 banks had become 'too big to fail' is by now widely accepted. Here, the argument is that the bigger a bank, the bigger the systemic risk posed by its potential collapse, making it more likely that it will be bailed out by the government. Indeed, the desire to obtain such an implicit government guarantee served as a major incentive for bank mergers and acquisitions. Along these lines, Brewer and Jagtiani (2009) suggest that banks actually were willing to pay a hefty premium to become too big to fail. Again, government policy, implicitly and inadvertently, shaped bank behaviour. It also meant that big banks, relying on these implicit guarantees, engaged in riskier activities. This behaviour has drawn a lot of criticism. Aversion to it has propelled vociferous calls for reform. As President Obama put it, 'never again will the American taxpayer be held hostage by a bank that is "too big to fail"' (White House 2010). However, for many policymakers perhaps a more important consideration than the moral issues involved is that, given exploding government debt levels in the wake of the crisis bailouts, some institutions might just have become 'too big to save' for financially constrained governments (ICB 2011b: 125).

Other advocates of breaking up the banks, such as UK Business Secretary Vince Cable, focus on consumer protection and related competition issues, citing the intimidating market power of a small range of financial institutions. However, it is important to point out that the concentration of the financial sector differs quite significantly across jurisdictions. Nevertheless, this attitude is still remarkable as it clearly rejects the logic of 'big is beautiful' on which a large number of mergers and acquisitions in the global financial industry had been based in the run-up to the recent financial crisis. The irony, of course, is that it was precisely the actions of the British and other governments in response to the crisis that have led to an even higher concentration in the banking sector today. Finally, there are voices who suggest that deposits should be ring-fenced so that they are safe from banks' riskier activities. Indeed, often these issues can be interlinked. Take, for example, the distortive effects on competition of banks pursuing a 'too big to fail' strategy or the danger that these institutions' risk-taking activities can pose for ordinary customers' deposits.

Given the different rationales for breaking up the banks, it is not surprising that there are various models under discussion for how this idea could be taken forward. For example, we can distinguish between functional separation (akin to the separation between commercial and investment banking) and measures to limit the overall size and market share of banks. The underlying objectives differ. Whilst a functional separation is deemed important with regard to reducing the risks to which depositors (and taxpayers) are exposed, limiting market share is meant to create a more competitive environment and thus be more consumer-friendly. Nevertheless, there have also been suggestions that increased competition can contribute to achieving greater financial-sector stability (see e.g. ICB 2011a).

The idea of breaking up the banks is neither something new nor something that has been successfully done or effectively managed in the past. Of course, perhaps the best example for such a policy with regard to both functional separation and limiting the overall market shares of banks was the 1933 Banking Act. Yet, the lessons that can be learnt from this experience are not as straightforward and unproblematic as it seems at first glance. As the history of that Act has shown, the segmentation of the American banking market reduced the potential for efficiencies, leading to higher costs for consumers, the padding of bank profits and whole segments of society being excluded from the credit market (Rosenbluth and Schaap 2003). So, breaking up the banks does not necessarily create a more competitive and consumer-friendly environment. Indeed, at least in earlier periods, it was linked to the interests of unit banks, which feared competition from branch banking (White 1982). It also was not a policy that could withstand the test of time, especially given the resurgence of international capital mobility, as discussed in Chapter 2. In this earlier episode the legislation was subsequently weakened, only to be ultimately repealed. What current reform proposals should avoid is this never-ending loop of regulation and deregulation via regulative rule-making. To do so, they have to be more radical in terms of both their genesis and their intention. We discuss this in the next chapter.

Moreover, even in the case that policymakers agree on the advisability of breaking up banks along functional lines, there are possible variations in the extent to which this separation is implemented. In the run-up to the late-1920s financial crisis and early-1930s Depression, banks used customer deposits to purchase corporate shares that they had underwritten, not necessarily with the knowledge of these customers (Uchitelle 2010). Thus, given this context, policymakers opted for a full separation of investment banking from traditional deposit-taking banking with the 1933 Banking Act. The idea of separating the different functions of banks was also, perhaps paradoxically, at least notionally part of the trend towards universal banking – banks that combine commercial and investment functions – in the late 1990s and early 2000s. This was especially so after the collapse of the dotcom bubble in the early 2000s. Indeed, the move towards creating European-style universal banks in the USA led to increased calls for the establishment of so-called Chinese walls to prevent institutions from exploiting the conflicts of interest this would create (see e.g. Crockett et al. 2003). Whilst the Sarbanes–Oxley Act of 2002 put into place provisions to prevent, in particular, analysts' conflicts of interests, its overall impact on the structure of financial firms was limited. It was a much weaker policy than the measures enacted with the 1933 Banking Act. Sarbanes–Oxley did little to prevent the risk-taking activities of individual units within financial organizations at a time when these institutions expanded both the scale and the scope of their activities. The case of AIG, although it is not a bank, is illustrative in this regard. In AIG the London branch wrote the financial contracts whose losses pushed the whole company to the brink. In the end, it had to be bailed out by the US government.

Other advocates of banking reform favour the breaking up of banks based on some sort of market power or risk concentration criterion. Thus, for example, President Obama suggested the idea of a 'deposit cap to guard against too much risk being concentrated in a single bank' (White House 2010). In the UK, the Independent Commission on Banking (ICB), tasked with considering structural reforms to 'promote financial stability and competition' in the UK financial sector, has pursued similar lines of thought (ICB 2011a: part 2). Of course, until recently, the two aims of financial stability and competition were seen as rather conflictual, which partially explains increases in bank size in the run-up to the crisis. In the short run it was merging banks, not breaking them up, that was the more immediate policy response to the current crisis. Take, for example, the state-facilitated takeover of Bear Stearns in spring 2008 in the USA and a series of further mergers that followed in a number of jurisdictions including the UK. This is very similar to the aftermath of the Asian financial crisis, which witnessed a growing number of bank mergers and the consolidation of financial groups in the affected countries. Hence, breaking up banks has to be seen not only as a response to slowly accumulated market power, but also as a remedy for the adverse consequences of short-term crisis solutions in the past.

What is surprising, however, is that the different ways in which various domestic banking sectors are organized is little discussed in policy documents outlining reform proposals. Similarly, whilst for example the ICB Interim Report mounts a strong defence of the benefits of a universal banking structure, it talks relatively little about the historical origins of such a structure or the specificity of the UK banking market and economy more generally, apart from restating the importance of the financial sector to the overall economy (ICB 2011b). The wider point is that in so doing reform proposals fail to embrace the link between government and public policy and the evolution of bank activity which we think so important.

What also becomes clear if we look at the discourses evolving around banking reform in the UK and the USA is that policymakers are less concerned about abstract notions of market power than about a drop in lending, in particular to small and medium-sized enterprises, in the wake of the crisis. There are also some suggestions for breaking up banks not just by function or market share but also by country of origin, where bailout funds could come with the condition of increased domestic lending targets (Dewatripont and Rochet 2010). Nevertheless, in what is for those familiar with the work of Robert W. Cox a typical 'problem-solving' manner, these proposals can be challenged for focusing too much on the financial sector as it is and not on what it could and should be. Considerations of the more general relationship between finance and the economy are treated as a subordinate matter.

With regard to specific policy proposals with the intention of breaking up the banks, or at least of limiting their size and the systemic risk they pose, two stand out: new international provisions for global systemically important financial institutions (SIFIs) and living wills. The issue of SIFIs is addressed as part of the revisions of the Basel framework (Basel III). More specifically, given that these institutions are deemed to pose a higher risk to the financial system, they will be required to hold more capital, in the range of an additional 1–2.5 percent (BCBS 2011). Living wills, or, to give them their formal title, 'recovery and resolution plans', require banks to draw up action plans for the case that a bank should endure duress or would have to be wound down. Both measures are intended to address the too-big-to-fail problem, the former by putting a surcharge on SIFIs which should counter-act the cost benefits that these institutions obtain from implicit government guarantees, the latter by sending strong signals that governments would be prepared to let go under even big financial institutions so long as certain safeguards are in place.

While breaking up the banks could be seen as a constitutive rule in that it has structural implications for the activities that banks of various types will be allowed to undertake in the future, on its own it does little to counteract the synchronic nature of contemporary banking. It does little in terms of (re)defining the purpose of banking, commercial and otherwise. It also does not help to refocus bank lending away from consumption and speculation towards investment in productivity improvement (see Montgomerie 2006). If we take seriously Leander's claim about the limited potential of the financial reform process, it comes as no surprise that proposals to break up the banks exhibit little originality. Moreover, it is questionable whether there is likely to be the political mobilization to turn this into a more radical solution and to move beyond regulatory devices such as the new Basel provisions for SIFIs and living wills, especially in the UK and the USA, which, although most exposed to the financial crisis, remain in thrall to financial sectors which have such a massive share of their respective economies. The trend seems to go rather in the other direction.

The Problem with Macroprudential Policies

Whilst the previous two policy measures are mainly targeted at individual financial institutions, macroprudential policymaking (MPP) is ostensibly targeted at the financial system as a whole. The idea behind macroprudential regulation is that, while individual financial institutions may appear sound, in a specific sector or sectors of the financial system risk could still accumulate to an extent where the whole sector comes under threat. In other words, the core rationale of MPP is the notion that strategic actions that are rational for individual organizations can collectively threaten the stability of and inflict harm on the financial system as a whole. The recent financial crisis exposed a number of such practices and their shortcomings. Most importantly, value-at-risk (VAR) models left financial institutions ill prepared once the economic situation deteriorated (see e.g. Best 2010). The risk of sudden unexpected price movements – 'tail risk' – was much bigger than anticipated. Accounting practices, more specifically so-called fair value accounting where the prices of assets and liabilities are marked to the market (i.e. current prices), served to amplify the crisis once the global financial system was on the downturn, as it forced institutions to mark down their balance sheets drastically and thus contributed to the downward spiral.

MPP is seen as an important policy instrument to prevent similar occurrences in the future. As Jean Tirole (2010: 58) put it, 'accounting is not a simple financial thermometer; it is not neutral with respect to economic behaviour. Economists will have to burrow into the detail of macroprudential monitoring, a major challenge for regulation.' Echoing this view, the Independent Commission on Banking in the UK answers its own question of 'How to make the system safer for the future?' with the following statement: 'An important part of the answer is better macroeconomic – including 'macro-prudential' – policy so that there are fewer and smaller shocks to the system' (ICB 2011c: 1–2). Indeed, the professional community of economists seems to be increasingly taken by the idea of MPP (Baker 2010). In this regard, the focus on MPP presents a reversal of economic thinking with a renewed focus on the links between macroeconomics and microeconomics, even though these are still seen as being analytically distinct (see Best and Widmaier 2006).

However, let us first establish the intellectual lineages of the idea of MPP, also in order to assess its potential to provide a more inclusive approach to regulatory norm formation. According to most accounts, MPP originated from within the core of financial policymaking circles. More specifically, the genesis of macroprudential policy proposals, in their current form, is usually traced back to an initiative of the Bank for International Settlements (BIS) (Clement 2010). It is said to have then taken BIS economists the better part of the last decade, until the global financial crisis offered a more fertile ground for this new regulatory approach, to convince fellow policymakers of its supposed effectiveness (Baker 2010). In practice, macroprudential regulation closely resembles the more pragmatic regulatory approaches of, for example, Spain and some East Asian jurisdictions. Potentially, it can include measures such as variable reserve requirements or credit restrictions to certain sectors or for certain products in order to dampen euphoria. In so doing, MPP perhaps represents a radical departure from the way financial systems in the UK and USA have been regulated. For other parts of Europe, such as Spain, and for much of East Asia, including Korea and Taiwan, it is not as innovative as its advocates claim.

Piet Clement (2010: 63) suggests that the Asian financial crisis of 1997–98 actually was the trigger for the term 'macroprudential' being used outside the small circle of BIS economists and policymakers. Nevertheless, in so doing he implies that this was an outside–in phenomenon, the international financial policy community picking up on the need for MPP. He ignores the application of policy measures that would now probably be subsumed under the notion of MPP by Asian financial policymakers in the wake of the 1997–98 crisis. Thus, discussions of MPP on the global level seem to consolidate a USA/UK-centred financial paradigm, at least in terms of the prevalent agenda-setting and decision-making structures when it comes to norm formation. Indeed, what is remarkable is that despite the challenge that the crisis has presented to the leadership role of the US and UK financial systems, there has largely been a conspicuous absence of non-Western voices and practices when it comes to reform proposals. This is the more surprising as other regions have had a long experience with financial crises and have experimented with numerous resolution mechanisms and longer-term reforms. Yet there seems to be little (and late) policy learning in the core economies from the experiences of other countries, as is demonstrated by the case of the already existing de facto macroprudential regulation in many Asian countries (*Financial Times*, 27 July 2010).

MPP has emerged as a new global financial norm, endorsed by the G20. It has already become a core part of the newly emerging regulatory architecture, especially with regard to the policies pursued by the Financial Stability Board (FSB) created in April 2009. Of course, this should not come as a surprise, given the close links between the FSB and the BIS. However, the view that more attention has to be paid to financial-sector developments more generally has already been obvious for a while with the introduction in 1999 of Financial Sector Assessment Programmes (FSAPs) by the IMF and the World Bank marking a high point (Moschella 2012). Nevertheless, global efforts are now to be mirrored also on the domestic level, which means a transformation of domestic regulatory infrastructures. The new focus on MPP also has to be seen as part of the new trend to focus on the development of domestic financial architectures that took hold more widely in the wake of the Asian financial crisis.

In terms of policy impact, the notion of MPP has to be broken down into its two core elements: its supervisory and regulatory dimensions. More specifically, in terms of supervision MPP marks a departure from the pre-crisis approach in that individual financial institutions are no longer the sole focus of supervisors. In terms of regulation, MPP suggests the possibility of introducing a whole range of new regulatory measures that will expand regulatory toolkits, especially of those countries that discarded so many of their traditional regulatory tools over the last two decades. Nevertheless, with regard to the regulatory responses associated with MPP, part of the problem is the ill-defined issue of what exactly constitutes MPP and what does not. In this regard, it is important to acknowledge that the term 'macroprudential regulation' is used to refer to a range of sometimes very different policy measures.

How the norm of MPP is taken forward in concrete terms is vital. MPP has received the most attention on a global scale as one of the two main thrusts of reforming the Basel framework (the other being improved micro-prudential, or perhaps rather bank-level, reform). Here, macroprudential reform is mainly understood as building up additional capital buffers to protect 'the banking sector in periods of excess aggregate credit growth' (BCBS 2011: 7). The idea is that in so doing the build-up of system-wide risks and their procyclical amplification can be reduced. However, as in the case of the SIFIs, it is remarkable that with this so-called macroprudential reform sector-wide issues are still meant to be tackled by regulating the conduct of individual institutions. With regard to the constitutive versus regulative nature of bank regulation, MPP scores rather low. Its advocates suggest that MPP has a 'cross-sectional dimension' that focuses on 'how risk was distributed within the financial system at any point in time' by concentrating 'on institutions having similar exposures within the financial system and the interconnections between these institutions' (Clement 2010: 64). However, in terms of actual policy responses, as indicated by the revised Basel III framework, requiring banks to increase capital buffers during good times, more specifically to demand that they build up additional equity between 0 and 2.5 per cent when authorities deem credit growth as excessive (BCBS 2011: 58), does not on its own reshape the identity of banks. Instead, it shows that regulation is still seen as external to what banks do, merely as a constraint on their conduct. In so doing, it fails to embrace the constitutive role of regulation and falls short of more radical measures such as breaking up the banks. Indeed, its advocates suggest that MPP will allow us both to have our cake and to eat it, with not just fewer but also less severe shocks. Nevertheless, this would be very much contingent on a bigger set of supporting reforms.

In terms of our schematic framework, MPP scores much better on the synchronic–diachronic axis than the previous two reform proposals. Indeed, MPP explicitly acknowledges the 'time dimension' of financial regulation (Borio 2003). More specifically, staff at the BIS have done the intellectual groundwork to frame MPP as a countermeasure to the procyclicality of the financial system and the way it was regulated in the run-up to the recent financial crisis. MPP calls for financial institutions to build up capital cushions during good times that could then be drawn down during bad times. In so doing, MPP is thought to act as a stabilizer. However, it is important to recognize that only some of the synchronic tendencies of global financial markets are addressed. Most significantly, the issue of financial market participant and bank executive compensation is ignored within this framework. Given the vast differences in private- and public-sector pay scales, this is also important when it comes to considering the regulatory capacity that is necessary to implement the macroprudential provisions of Basel III and other reforms successfully. Similarly, it is doubtful whether on its own it will be sufficient to encourage banks to pursue more productive and/or sustainable lending practices that would truly move them into the reflexive banking category of quadrant 1.

An often ignored aspect of the move to MPP is that it will give rise to capacity issues closely related to the new demands that it puts on domestic financial infrastructures, especially as the proposals discussed would have different impacts in different parts of the world. A common denominator in the run-up to the recent global financial crisis was the decline in regulatory capacity in both material (i.e. reductions in staff and other resources) and ideational terms (as articulated in the 'the market knows best' paradigm), especially so in the core economies. This is hardly reconcilable with a move towards MPP, which will require increased resources. Thus, by committing to MPP, countries around the world also have to commit to strengthening regulatory resources to make this step meaningful. Apart from the shift in thinking that this requires in the core economies, most importantly the USA and the UK, both subject to austerity budgets, it will also negatively affect less developed countries by putting additional pressure on scarce resources. To put it briefly, there are a number of unresolved issues when it comes to the introduction of MPP on both domestic and global levels that will require further thought.

In the boom years of the early 2000s, BIS efforts to promote MPP did not receive much attention; neither did those stabilization policies that were pursued outside the Anglo-American core that bear close resemblance to what has now been reinvented as MPP. With regard to Leander's claim about the doxa of financial policymaking limiting the possibilities of financial reform, it is important to remember that BIS is a crucial node in the networks of international financial policymaking. There is some room for doxa to evolve over time, and the broader acceptance of MPP since the outbreak of the global financial crisis certainly supports this notion, but reform discussions still seem limited. There is little acknowledgement of the politics involved. The range of options remains limited, with the allegation of a proposal being unprofessional still being lethal. Whilst its advocates could make the case for MPP being a serious reform proposal, the fallacious framing of MPP as a near panacea to the problems that befell financial institutions over the last decade indicates that policymakers significantly underestimate the constitutive character of regulation and how it shapes the behaviour of banks.

Conclusion

Post-crisis bank regulation is hampered by the view that all that regulators can do is to impose rules on the conduct of banks, and even that only to a fairly limited extent. In purely material terms, the view that if regulators come down too hard on the banking sector, banks would relocate to other jurisdictions is widespread and has drawn the sting of reform proposals, at least in the UK. Similarly, the more intellectual argument that an increasingly hands-on approach to bank regulation would push banking activities into the shadow banking sector and thus increase risk and lessen overall regulatory control prevails in financial policymaking circles. The recent global financial crisis certainly did not provide us with the impetus for a drastic shift in regulatory attitudes. Indeed, this holds true for the field of global governance more generally (see e.g. Broome et al. 2012 and contributions to the special issue; Sinclair 2012).

In this chapter, we have explored a range of reform proposals that have been mooted in financial policymaking circles in the USA and Europe, as well as on the global level. For this purpose, we have looked at three issue areas in greater detail: attempts to ban proprietary trading; further-reaching efforts to break up the banks in terms of both function and market share; and the new focus on macroprudential policymaking. We suggest that all these proposals ignore the constitutive role played by government when it comes to shaping the nature of banks, although to varying degrees. Regulation continues to be perceived (wrongly) as being external to how banks operate, constraining their conduct, not shaping their behaviour. Both banning proprietary trading and breaking up the banks fail to address the increasingly synchronic logic of financial markets and the way that banks operate. Macroprudential policies, whilst ostensibly countercyclical in character, address only some of these issues. In sum, just breaking up banks, imposing limits on their size, applying the Volcker rule or creating mechanisms for improved macroprudential regulation are not sufficient to rid us of the problem with banks.

We concede that it is perhaps a little unfair to talk about these reform proposals individually, as they are often presented as part of a catalogue of reforms. However, if we situate these proposals within our schematic framework, then it becomes clear that, even in combination, they do not go far enough to move us towards a system of reflexive banking. In this regard, we concur with Leander's claim about the limited scope of the financial reform process, especially as, despite the coming to prominence of new forums such as the G20 (established in 1999 but only catapulted to global attention in 2008), there has not been a radical transformation of who sets the agenda and makes the decisions.

Indeed, it is questionable whether in these circumstances the problem with banks can ever be addressed adequately. Instead, in the next chapter, we suggest that a more incisive view of change is needed, which relates to the very purpose of banking institutions and financial policymaking and its social legitimacy.

CONCLUSION

WHAT IS TO BE DONE
ABOUT BANKS?

The problem with banks is one of the key political issues we face in the second decade of the twenty-first century. As we have shown in this book, banks are not the ordered, sensible institutions those who run them and those who regulate them suggest them to be most of the time. Time and again through history these critical institutions have let us down, creating major problems for all who need to keep their money safe or to borrow. Given this, it is surely amazing that there have been so few periods of sustained investigation and reform of banks such as in the 1930s. We think, given the effects of the global financial crisis that started in 2007, that this is the time for serious thought and action about what is to be done about banks. Oddly, as it seems to us, relatively few people in the policymaking world have thought in these terms, despite the economic and financial carnage of the last few years. They appear much happier with quick fixes that paper over the most obvious cracks, leaving a fundamentally volatile system unchanged.

As we see it, the thought that has gone into the problem with banks has been almost entirely focused on rethinking regulation, understood as being external to actual bank behaviour. Many investigative reports and policy briefs have been produced by agencies in the United States and Europe going into thousands of printed pages. Some are still in progress. These are surely very worthy and in most cases the implementation of their ideas would help to deal with some of the issues created by banks. They do not, however, deal with the problem with banks as we have presented it in this book. Most importantly, they do not deal with the purpose of these institutions, as we set this out in Figure 1.1. Now it is easy to say that the purpose of capitalist institutions is to produce a profit and that is that. But this position does not account for the systemic quality of banks – the fact that the actions of large banks can imperil the whole system; nor does this view acknowledge the historically variable organization and purposes of banking institutions. Banks vary, just as apples do. Braeburn, Jazz and Cox's apple varieties are all apples, but quite different from each other. Citibank is very different in scale and range of activities to a local savings-and-loan bank.

Asserting continuity will not shield us from volatility or give us the banks that do what we want them to do. As consumers of apples, we already know we do not like Braeburns; they gave us a serious stomach upset; but having recovered from a nasty bout we are still being offered them and nothing else. Things have changed greatly in the banking and financial markets in the last decade. The impulse of our policymakers to return to the status quo ante makes rather implausible assumptions about the ease with which we will regain stability. We all think financial markets have changed and that they are now more animated by Keynes's animal spirits than ever. The assumptions built into banks and proposed regulation do not incorporate this reality, seeing the Great Panic as an aberrant moment rather than a reality of the social foundations of modern banking.

In what follows we set out what we think are the three fundamental insights about banks. We appreciate that making these ideas real raises a big problem that all social change faces, that of agency. We cannot offer even a tentative solution to this problem in the confines of a book like this. What we fear is that the sort of change we advocate will only come about in the most dreadful circumstances, like those faced in the 1930s. Such circumstances are certainly not beyond the feasible at the time of writing. If the worst does come to pass we would expect to see ideas like these enjoy a new popularity.

Banks Have Changed beyond Recognition

Banks have always faced major challenges. As we discussed in Chapter 2, they borrow short in the form of deposits and lend long as loans. Depositors can demand their cash back at any time, but in order to pay interest to depositors and cover the costs of operations banks rarely have more than a fraction of these deposits on hand – not much more than just enough to cover the demands of depositors on a day-to-day basis, plus some (as little as possible) in reserve. Managing this basic contradiction between short-term liabilities and long-term assets is key to survival for any bank, as a rumour that the bank is in trouble can precipitate a bank run by desperate depositors, as UK-based Northern Rock experienced in September 2007.

But we should not exaggerate the timelessness of banking. Banks have been put under pressure in recent years by cheaper and multiple sources of funding. Whether we ascribe this to the global spread of American financial norms or to globalization does not matter. What does is that capital and money markets have eaten into the business model of banks in the developed world. Some people wrote off the banks twenty years ago, suggesting they were a dying breed and would soon become extinct. But this proved to be premature. Banks are determined institutions and they too made use of the capital markets for their own ends. Deposit-taking institutions sought to make use of the securities markets, for their customers, but most importantly for themselves, through proprietary trading. By doing so, staid commercial and retail banks like Bank of America and HSBC changed identity and became much more like Goldman Sachs, an institution known for risky and complex market stratagems. The banks we grew up with, where the bank manager only gave loans to very well-documented borrowers, became something else, as they demonstrated in the years prior to the global financial crisis that started in 2007.

So banks are not what they were in Europe or in America. It is likely in time these changes to a more volatile form may be pursued in Asia as well. The problem with this transformation is that we are not talking about car washes or Internet service providers, where competition is keen, there are many of them and it does not matter too much if some go out of business. For most businesses and certainly most individuals there are relatively few banks to choose from as places to keep our money, such as it is. Those that exist are often deemed by the authorities 'too big to fail' and thus to be supported in the event of a loss of confidence. Ironically, then, a critical societal infrastructure – banks – in which we store and transfer our resources has been heavily involved in the most extreme forms of financial innovation, driven by the hunt for yield. This dynamic is a bit like fitting a Formula One racing car engine to all family sedans and then wondering why so many cars seem to go out of control, crash and burn. Given the importance of banks for our welfare, how they have changed character and behaviour, and the risks some of their activities in recent years have posed to the financial system and thus to us all, we conclude it would be foolish to live with the current arrangements. A regulatory 'slap on the wrist', as seems to be proposed, will not save us from the problem with banks.

We Are Responsible for What Banks Do

The odd thing about the relationship between states and banks is that although, as we have seen, states focus on problem-solving change via regulatory reform, what states do has profound consequences for what banks are. Although state initiatives tend to be piecemeal and are often outmanoeuvred by the banks' regulatory arbitrage (for example, special-purpose vehicles and other off-balance sheet activities), the effect, in aggregate, is unconsciously to shape the very constitution of banks, or what banks are and what they do. The dominant trend over the last two decades towards synchronic banking under regulative rules (quadrant III in Figure 1.1), which has challenged other configurations in a range of countries, has been encouraged by regulation such as the Basel agreements. Regulation has simply assumed that the purpose of banking is limited to maximizing profit in the short run, and not challenged these objectives. A rules-based approach, which appears to be where post-crisis regulation is heading, is likely to further this assumption, as the guiding principle here is that whatever is not forbidden is permissible. Although that seems to provide little guidance, it actually serves to reinforce the pervasiveness of the synchronic/regulative model.

The best we can say for the explicit relationship between states and banks is that it has been one governed by ordoliberal concepts, which assume the market depends on a legal and institutional framework governed by rules (Vanberg 2011: 5). This way of thinking has been popularized in recent years by Williamson (1985). We are dubious about the merits of this approach because it remains a fundamentally elite-driven project. It reproduces the idea that banking and finance more generally constitute a technical sphere where great expertise is needed in order to make correct decisions. That means public discussion and determination of policy choices is ruled illegitimate. But we think the events of recent times show that more than expertise is necessary to make banking work for the good of all. Public engagement with banking is necessary, as the British deputy prime minister has suggested (Wintour 2011). As Thirkell-White has indicated, state–bank relations, and indeed all regulatory programmes, imply consequences for both efficiency and equity. The appropriate trade-off or mix between the two is not something expertise can offer insight on: 'there is no single "best" solution to regulatory questions' (Thirkell-White 2009: 690).

Like Thirkell-White, we believe a broader public debate of banking policy is essential (Thirkell-White 2009: 706). Shiller has suggested there must be what he calls a democratizing of finance via regulation so that ordinary people can plan for their futures with the same tools as those used by the elite (Shiller 2011: 4). This might apply, he notes, in real estate, which is the major financial investment made by most people, but which is illiquid, unlike the markets that those with real wealth enjoy (Shiller 2011: 31). He thinks part of this agenda is making banks acknowledge how people actually plan and anticipate risk. Fairness (or legitimacy) is a crucial determinant, suggests Shiller, as to whether regulation will succeed or fail (Shiller 2011: 6).

While Shiller's agenda appeals to us, it does not go far enough in our view. As we see it, a wider set of options should be on the table for public deliberation. The big questions should be asked. Key among these is the issue of whether contemporary banking, of the quadrant III variety, actually serves a purpose other than to enrich the bankers involved. In other words, is it 'socially worthless' (Cassidy 2010: 49)? Not all financial innovation is good. Some of it, like asset-backed securities, is inefficient because it undermines the processes that should reinforce the quality of the risks taken. More importantly, if banking is systemically risky, as it has shown itself to be, and not just for finance but for the economy and society as a whole, then there must be a systemic and social benefit to the activity. If not, we are simply underwriting rent-seeking rather than something of any real value.

Banks Can Work for Us

We have three more specific ideas to make banks resemble the institution we would like them to be. These ideas would, in conjunction with what we have said about decision-making, push banks back towards the constitutive–diachronic quadrant depicted in Figures 1.1 and 5.1, although we recognize that the problem with banks may never be fully solved, or reflexive, responsible banking created given the current financial doxa. More specifically, we suggest that in debating banking reform we can learn from alternative banking models, such as Islamic finance; other industries such as commercial passenger plane manufacturing and the global pharmaceuticals industry; and other professions such as lawyers and medical practitioners.

Banking in developed countries can learn from other systems. At present, banks engage in a game of trying to specify, control and pass on risk. This is very much in keeping with contract law, which allocates specific responsibilities to contracting parties and provides for penalties for failure to meet the terms of the contract. But the role of asset-backed securities in the global financial crisis demonstrates some of the problems inherent in a risk-transfer system in which originators of mortgages were able to free themselves of the original credit risk in liquid markets. This undermined scrutiny of creditworthiness, contributing to the sorry saga of financial mayhem. What if a more responsible approach were taken? This is where the idea of sharing in risk, taken from Islamic finance, may be a useful approach (Rethel 2011). In this system, borrowers and lenders share in the benefits (and losses) of investment. This approach is less synchronic as it extends the time horizon, perhaps over years. It is constitutive because lenders have a strong interest in the organization of borrowers. The two parties do not face each other as hostile parties, but as partners in a common enterprise.

We need a safe system that is less likely to suffer the sort of crises endemic to global finance since Bretton Woods. Part of that no doubt is acknowledging what Shiller calls the human dimension to financial behaviour. It might also be possible for banking to learn from other industries. Bankers have historically objected to regulation, as have other industries, suggesting there is a trade-off between innovation and safety. Two industries suggest this trade-off can be better managed than has been the case in banking in recent years. Commercial passenger plane manufacture is one. The other is the global pharmaceuticals industry. Both are highly innovative spheres which have massive effects on welfare. Safety is key to enterprise success in each industry. Perhaps that should be so in banking? There could perhaps be something akin to the annual inspection of an automobile as roadworthy, or a more accountable version of the credit rating process that has rated commercial and sovereign securities for decades. Perhaps peer review might work better than external inspection, given the crucial question of the calibre and incentives of those who review. Other things being equal, we think an emphasis on safety standards, rather than just meeting minimum regulatory rules, would make a lot of sense and bring about a strengthening in banks and what they do. Just as car manufacturers like Volvo and Saab sell their cars in part based on safety features, banks too could identify how they keep your money safe and why this is the best approach to safeguarding your savings.

Our last idea about how to make banks work for us is to encourage different cultural norms in the industry. Airline pilots and scientists working in pharmaceuticals could be our guide, but so could many other professionals. Although both operate in a strongly regulated culture, their respective professions place a great deal of responsibility on their shoulders. Simply obeying the rules (synchronic–regulative) is not enough in a professional culture (diachronic–constitutive) and we think reforms of this nature would be an appealing direction for banking. One way to achieve this might be to institutionalize the profession of banker, at first in deposit-taking institutions, who might be required to achieve specified educational and training qualifications and be certified as right and proper persons, in the way that lawyers and medical practitioners are. Although the promotion of a trustee-ship culture sounds expensive, it seems merited to us given the systemic risk banks pose to society, as revealed in the global financial crisis that began in 2007.

Conclusion

The problem with banks is not going away any time soon. Banks are rich, problematic and often fast-moving institutions guided by a highly individualist financial doxa which maximizes their freedom of action in the interests of the efficiency of the self-regulating market. However, as Polanyi showed, this is a utopian vision of self-reliant institutions coming together to produce maximum benefit (Polanyi 1957). When things do not work out so well, when financial euphoria turns into a Great Panic, utopia becomes dystopia. This does not occur by chance. It happens because of the parameters set out in Figure 1.1.

A key implication of this book is that banks are under great stress. What they do and how they do it have changed greatly in recent years in response to long-run pressure on their business model. In coming to an understanding of the problem with banks we need to appreciate that banks have been driven to change as much as they have sought it themselves. States have encouraged this development, seeing the chance for greater efficiency and improved performance in the banking sector. States help make banks, and do not just regulate them.

What has been neglected in all this is the other side of systemic risk: the collective responsibility we all share to make a useful and viable industry out of banking that serves our purposes. After all, if banking only serves its own interests, then it is merely a rent-seeker, given the wider social costs demonstrated by the global financial crisis that began in 2007.

Given what we said above about states making banks, there is every reason to be confident about the potential for remaking banks and, at least partially, alleviating the problem with banks. We acknowledge the problem with agency. But we think banks represent quite a risky phenomenon to states after 2007. If states ignore public anger about banks and their role in the financial meltdown they risk reducing confidence in future prosperity. So we think states, as the makers of banks, have some interest in being the remakers of them too. Whether this is minimalist or something more substantive we think is likely to be determined by further traumas produced by the problem with banks and the public dissent from the prevailing financial doxa this is likely to generate.

REFERENCES

Adrian, Tobias, and Hyun Song Shin (2010) 'The Changing Nature of Financial Intermediation and the Financial Crisis of 2007–2009', *Annual Review of Economics*, pp. 603–18.

Akerlof, George A., and Robert J. Shiller (2009) *Animal Spirits; How Human Psychology Drives the Economy and Why It Matters for Global Capitalism*, Princeton NJ and Oxford: Princeton University Press.

Amyx, Jennifer (2004) *Japan's Financial Crisis: Institutional Rigidity and Reluctant Change*, Princeton NJ and Oxford: Princeton University Press.

Asian Development Bank (2011) AsianBondsOnline database – Domestic Financial Profiles, http://asianbondsonline.adb.org/regional/data/bondmarket. php?code=Domestic_Financing_profile; accessed 10 November 2011.

Bachmann, Mark (1990) Testimony of Mark Bachmann, Senior Vice President, Corporate Finance Department, Standard & Poor's Ratings Group, 'High Yield Debt Market/Junk Bonds', hearing before the Subcommittee on Telecommunications and Finance of the Committee on Energy and Commerce, House of Representatives, 101st Congress, second session, 8 March 1990, Washington DC: US Government Printing Office.

Bagehot, Walter (1873) *Lombard Street: A Description of the Money Market*, 3rd edn, London: Henry, S. King.

Bailey, Fenton (1991) *The Junk Bond Revolution: Michael Milken, Wall Street and the Roaring Eighties*, London: Fourth Estate.

Baker, Andrew (2010) 'Financial Booms, Crisis Politics and Macroprudential Regulation: The Political Economy of an Ideational Shift', paper presented at the AGORA workshop on Global Knowledge Networks, Brown University, Providence RI, 21–22 June.

Baker, Dean (2009) *Plunder and Blunder: The Rise and Fall of the Bubble Economy*, Sausalito CA: PoliPoint Press.

Bank of England (2007) *Financial Stability Report*, London, October.

Banner, Stuart B. (1998) *Anglo-American Securities Regulation: Cultural and Political Roots, 1690–1860*, Cambridge: Cambridge University Press.

BCBS (2011) 'Basel III: A Global Regulatory Framework for More Resilient Banks and Banking Systems', revised version, June 2011, www.bis.org/publ/bcbs189. htm; accessed 18 November 2011.

Best, Jacqueline (2010) 'The Limits of Financial Risk Management: Or, What We Didn't Learn from the Asian Crisis', *New Political Economy* 15(1), pp. 29–49.

Best, Jacqueline, and Wesley Widmaier (2006) 'Micro- or Macro-Moralities? International Economic Discourses and Policy Possibilities', *Review of International Political Economy* 13(4), pp. 609–33.

Blundell-Wignall, Adrian (2007) 'Structured Products: Implications for Financial Markets', *Financial Market Trends* 93(2), pp. 29–57.

Blundell-Wignall, Adrian, Gert Wehinger and Patrick Slovik (2009) 'The Elephant in the Room: The Need to Deal with What Banks Do', *Financial Market Trends* 2009(2), pp. 11–35.

Borio, Claudio (2003) 'Towards a Macroprudential Framework for Financial Supervision and Regulation?', BIS Working Papers No. 128, www.bis.org/ publ/work128.pdf; accessed 18 July 2011.

Brewer, Elijah, and Julapa Jagtiani (2009) 'How Much Did Banks Pay to Become Too-big-to-fail and to Become Systemically Important?', *Working Papers 09-34*, Federal Reserve Bank of Philadelphia, www.philadelphiafed. org/research-and-data/publications/working-papers/2009/wp09-34.pdf.

Broome, André, Liam Clegg and Lena Rethel (2012) 'Global Governance and the Politics of Crisis', *Global Society* 26(1), pp. 3–17.

Bruner, Robert F., and Sean D. Carr (2007) *The Panic of 1907: Lessons Learned from the Market's Perfect Storm*, New York: Wiley.

Busch, Andreas (2009) *Banking Regulation and Globalization*, Oxford: Oxford University Press.

Carter, Adrienne, and Ben Protess (2011) 'UBS Scandal is a Reminder of Why Dodd-Frank Came to Be', *New York Times*, 19 September.

Cassidy, John (2010) 'What Good is Wall Street?' *The New Yorker*, 29 November, pp. 49–57.

CGFS (Committee on the Global Financial System) (2003) *Credit Risk Transfer*, Report submitted by a working group established by the Committee on the Global Financial System, January, www.bis.org/publ/cgfs20.pdf; accessed 17 July 2011.

Cheng Linsun (2003) *Banking in Modern China: Entrepreneurs, Professional Managers, and the Development of Chinese Banks, 1897–1937*, Cambridge: Cambridge University Press.

Clement, Piet (2010) 'The Term "Macroprudential", Origins and Evolution', *BIS Quarterly Review*, March, pp. 59–67.

Cook, Malcolm (2008) *Banking Reform in Southeast Asia*, London: Routledge.

Cox, Robert W., with Timothy J. Sinclair (1996). *Approaches to World Order*. Cambridge: Cambridge University Press.

Crockett, Andrew, et al. (2003) *Conflicts of Interest in the Financial Services Industry: What Shall We Do About Them?*, Geneva: International Centre for Monetary and Banking Studies.

Crouch, Colin (2009) 'Privatised Keynesianism: An Unacknowledged Policy Regime', *British Journal of Politics and International Relations* 11(3), pp. 382–99.

Davies, Howard, and David Green (2010) *Global Financial Regulation: The Essential Guide*, Cambridge: Polity Press.

Davis, William Stearns (1910) *The Influence of Wealth in Imperial Rome*, New York: Macmillan.

Dewatripont, Mathias, and Jean-Charles Rochet (2010) 'The Treatment of Distressed Banks', in Mathias Dewatripont, Jean-Charles Rochet and Jean Tirole (eds), *Balancing the Banks*, Princeton NJ and Oxford: Princeton University Press, pp. 107–30.

Dewatripont, Mathias, Jean-Charles Rochet and Jean Tirole (2010) 'Introduction', in Mathias Dewatripont, Jean-Charles Rochet and Jean Tirole (eds), *Balancing the Banks*, Princeton NJ and Oxford: Princeton University Press, pp. 1–9.

De Goede, Marieke (2004) 'Repoliticising Financial Risk', *Economy and Society* 33(2), pp. 197–217.

Dow Jones (2009) www.djiindexes.com; accessed 3 March 2009.

Downes, John, and Jordan Elliot Goodman (1991) *Dictionary of Finance and Investment Terms*, New York: Barron's.

Economist, The (1992) 'Time to Leave: A Survey of World Banking', 2 May.

Economist, The (1994) 'Recalled to Life: A Survey of International Banking', 30 April.

Eichengreen, Barry J. (1996) *Golden Fetters: The Gold Standard and the Great Depression, 1919–1939*, Oxford: Oxford University Press.

Ertürk, Ismail, and Stefano Solari (2007) 'Banks as Continuous Reinvention', *New Political Economy* 12(3), pp. 369–88.

FDIC (Federal Deposit Insurance Corporation) (2011) 'Statistics at a Glance', www.fdic.gov/bank/statistical/stats/2010dec/industry.html; accessed 17 July 2011.

Federal Reserve (2011) *Flow of Funds Accounts of the United States*, Washington DC: Board of Governors of the Federal Reserve System.

Ferguson, Niall (2009) 'Wall Street's New Gilded Age', *Newsweek*, 11 September, www.newsweek.com/2009/09/10/wall-street-s-new-gilded-age.print.html; accessed 9 October 2009.

Foot, Rosemary, and Andrew Walter (2010) *China, the United States and Global Order*, Oxford: Oxford University Press.

Frieden, Jeffry A. (1987) *Banking on the World: The Politics of International Finance*, New York: Blackwell.

Froud, Julie, Michael Moran, Adriana Nilsson and Karel Williams (2010) 'Wasting a Crisis? Democracy and Markets in Britain after 2007', *Political Quarterly* 81(1), pp. 25–38.

FSA (2008) *The Supervision of Northern Rock: A Lessons Learnt Review*, Internal Audit Division, www.fsa.gov.uk/pubs/other/nr_report.pdf; accessed 17 July 2011.

Galbraith, John Kenneth (1977) *The Age of Uncertainty*, London: Trafalgar.

Galbraith, John Kenneth (1993) *A Short History of Financial Euphoria*, Harmondsworth: Penguin.

Galbraith, John Kenneth (1997) *The Great Crash 1929*, New York: Mariner.

Gamble, Andrew (2009) *The Spectre at the Feast*, Basingstoke: Palgrave Macmillan.

Germain, Randall (2010) *Global Politics and Financial Governance*, Basingstoke: Palgrave Macmillan.

Goldstein, Morris, David Folkerts-Landau, Mohamed El-Erian, Steven Fries and Liliana Rojas-Suarez (1992) *International Capital Markets: Developments, Prospects, and Policy Issues*, Washington DC: International Monetary Fund.

Government of Malaysia (1999) *Status of the Malaysian Economy*, White Paper, Kuala Lumpur: Dewan Rakyat Printer.

Grant, James (1990) Testimony of James Grant, Grant's Interest Rate Observer, 'High Yield Debt Market/Junk Bonds', hearing before the Subcommittee on Telecommunications and Finance of the Committee on Energy and Commerce, House of Representatives, 101st Congress, second session, 8 March 1990, Washington DC: US Government Printing Office.

Grant, James (1992) *Money of the Mind: Borrowing and Lending in America from the Civil War to Michael Milken*, New York: Farrar Straus Giroux.

Grossman, Richard S. (2010) *Unsettled Account: The Evolution of Banking in the Industrialized World since 1800*, Princeton NJ and Oxford: Princeton University Press.

Haggard, Stephan (1990) *Pathways from the Periphery: The Politics of Growth in the Newly Industrializing Countries*, Ithaca and London: Cornell University Press.

Haggard, Stephan (2000) *The Political Economy of the Asian Financial Crisis*, Washington: IIE.

Hamilton-Hart, Natasha (2002) *Asian States, Asian Bankers: Central Banking in Southeast Asia*, Ithaca and London: Cornell University Press.

Hardie, Iain, and David Howarth (2011) 'Market-Based Banking and the Financial Crisis', Working Paper, www.pol.ed.ac.uk/__data/assets/pdf_file/0004/64561/HardieHowarthMMBFinal32011.pdf ; accessed 22 June 2011.

Harmes, Adam (1998) 'Institutional Investors and the Reproduction of Neoliberalism', *Review of International Political Economy* 5(1), pp. 92–121.

Hartmann, Philipp, Angela Maddaloni and Simone Manganelli (2003) 'The Euro Area Financial System: Structure, Integration and Policy Initiatives', ECB Working Paper No. 230.

Helleiner, Eric, and Stefano Pagliari (2011) 'The End of an Era in International Financial Regulation? A Postcrisis Research Agenda', *International Organization* 65(1), pp. 169–200.

Herring, Richard J. (2005) 'BCCI & Barings: Bank Resolutions Complicated by Fraud and Global Corporate Structure', in Doug Evanoff and George Kaufman (eds), *Systemic Financial Crises: Resolving Large Bank Insolvencies*, Hackensack NJ: World Scientific Publishing, pp. 321–45.

Hickman, W. Braddock (1958) *Corporate Bond Quality and Investor Experience*, Princeton NJ and Oxford: Princeton University Press.

Hildreth, Richard (2001) *The History of Banks* [1837], Kitchener ON: Batoche Books.

Hill, Hal (2003) 'East Asia in Crisis: Overview of the Key Issues', *Australian Economic History Review* 43(2), pp. 115–24.

HM Treasury (2008) *Resource Accounts 2007–8*, London: Stationery Office.

Hoggson, Noble Foster (1926) *Banking through the Ages: From the Romans to the Rothschilds*, New York: Dodd, Mead.

Hutchcroft, Paul (1998) *Booty Capitalism. The Politics of Banking in the Philippines*, Ithaca NY: Cornell University Press.

ICB (Independent Commission on Banking) (2011a) *Final Report Recommendations*, September, http://bankingcommission.s3.amazonaws.com/wp-content/uploads/2010/07/ICB-Final-Report.pdf; accessed 18 November 2011.

ICB (Independent Commission on Banking) (2011b) *Interim Report*, 11 April, http://s3-eu-west-1.amazonaws.com/htcdn/Interim-Report-110411.pdf; accessed 22 June 2011.

ICB (Independent Commission on Banking) (2011c) *Interim Report*, Executive Summary, 11 April 11, http://s3-eu-west-1.amazonaws.com/htcdn/Interim-Report-110411.pdf; accessed 22 June 2011.

Investment Company Institute (2011) *2011 Investment Company Factbook*, Washington DC: Investment Company Institute.

Ji Zhaojin (2003) *A Modern History of Shanghai Banking*, Armonk NY: M.E. Sharpe.

Johnson, Simon (2009) 'The Quiet Coup', *Atlantic Magazine*, www.theatlantic.com/magazine/archive/2009/05/the-quiet-coup/7364/; accessed 22 June 2011.

Johnson, Simon, and James Kwak (2010) *13 Bankers: The Wall Street Takeover and the Next Financial Meltdown*, New York: Pantheon.

Kane, Edward J. (1977) 'Good Intentions and Unintended Evil: The Case Against Selective Credit Allocation', *Journal of Money, Credit and Banking* 1(1), pp. 55–69.

Kapstein, Ethan B. (1989) 'Resolving the Regulator's Dilemma: International Coordination of Banking Regulations', *International Organization* 43(2), pp. 323–47.

Kapstein, Ethan B. (1992) 'Between Power and Purpose: Central Bankers and the Politics of Regulatory Convergence', *International Organization* 46(1), pp. 265–87.

Kindleberger, Charles P. (1993) *A Financial History of Western Europe*, 2nd edn, Oxford: Oxford University Press.

Kindleberger, Charles P. (2000) *Manias, Panics and Crashes: A History of Financial Crises*, 4th edn, Basingstoke: Palgrave Macmillan.

Kindleberger, Charles P., and Robert Z. Aliber (2005) *Manias, Panics and Crashes. A History of Financial Crises*, 5th edn, Basingstoke: Palgrave Macmillan.

King, Michael R. (2001) 'Who Triggered the Asian Financial Crisis?', *Review of International Political Economy* 8(3), pp. 438–66.

Kroszner, Randall S. (1998) 'Rethinking Bank Regulation. A Review of the Historical Evidence, *Journal of Applied Corporate Finance* 11(2), pp. 48–58.

Langley, Paul (2008) 'Sub-prime Mortgage Lending: A Cultural Economy', *Economy and Society* 37(4), pp. 469–94.

Leander, Anna (2009) 'Close Range: Targeting Regulatory Reform', *International Political Sociology* 3(4), pp. 465–8.

Lincoln, Bruce (1994) *Authority: Construction and Corrosion*, Chicago: University of Chicago Press.

Lukes, Steven (1974) *Power: A Radical View*, London: Macmillan.

MacKenzie, Donald (2006) *An Engine, Not a Camera: How Financial Models Shape Markets*, Boston MA: MIT Press.

Macpherson, Nicholas (2011) 'The Treasury and the Transition to the New Government', speech delivered at Nuffield College, Oxford, 18 June, www.hm-treasury.gov.uk/speech_permsec_180611.htm; accessed 10 November 2011.

Madrid, Raúl L. (1992) *Overexposed: US Banks Confront the Third World Debt Crisis*, Boulder CO: Westview Press.

Maurer, Bill (2005) *Mutual Life, Limited: Islamic Banking, Alternative Currencies, Lateral Reason*, Princeton NJ: Princeton University Press.

Miller, David (1991) 'Authority', in *The Blackwell Encyclopaedia of Political Thought*, ed. David Miller, Oxford: Blackwell, pp. 27–31.

Montgomerie, Johnna (2006) (2006) 'Financialisation of the American Credit Card Industry', *Competition and Change* 10(3), pp. 301–19.

Moschella, Manuela (2012) 'IMF Surveillance in Crisis The Past, Present, and Future of the Reform Process', *Global Society* 26(1), pp. 43–60.

Moshirian, Fariborz (2011) 'The Global Financial Crisis and the Evolution of Markets, Institutions and Regulation', *Journal of Banking & Finance* 35(3), pp. 502–11.

Mosley, Layna (2010) 'Regulating Globally, Implementing Locally: The Financial Codes and Standards Effort', *Review of International Political Economy* 17(4), pp. 724–61.

Mügge, Daniel (2010) *Widen the Market, Narrow the Competition*, Colchester: ECPR Press.

Mügge, Daniel (2011) 'From Pragmatism to Dogmatism: EU Governance, Policy Paradigms, and Financial Meltdown', *New Political Economy* 16(2), pp. 185–206.

Oatley, Thomas, and Robert Nabors (1998) 'Redistributive Cooperation: Market Failure, Wealth Transfers, and the Basle Accord', *International Organization* 52(1), pp. 35–54.

Obstfeld, Maurice, and Alan M. Taylor (2004) *Global Capital Markets: Integration, Crisis, Growth*, Cambridge: Cambridge University Press.

Palazzo, Guido, and Lena Rethel (2008) 'Conflicts of Interest in Financial Intermediation', *Journal of Business Ethics* 81(1), pp. 193–207.

Paulson, Henry (2010) *On the Brink: Inside the Race to Stop the Collapse of the Global Financial System*, New York: Business Plus.

Pilloff, Steven J. (2004) 'Bank Merger Activity in the United States, 1994–2003', Board of Governors of the Federal Reserve System, Staff Study 176, May.

Polanyi, Karl (1957) *The Great Transformation: Political and Economic Origins of Our Time* [1944], Boston MA: Beacon Press.

Power, Michael (2005) 'The Invention of Operational Risk', *Review of International Political Economy* 12(4), pp. 577–99.

Reinhart, Carmen, and Kenneth Rogoff (2008) 'Banking Crises: An Equal Opportunity Menace', NBER Working Paper 14587.

Reinhart, Carmen, and Kenneth Rogoff (2009) *This Time Is Different: Eight Centuries of Financial Folly*, Princeton NJ and Oxford: Princeton University Press.

Reinhart, Carmen, and Kenneth Rogoff (2011) 'This Time is Different – Data for Download', www.reinhartandrogoff.com/data/; accessed 18 November 2011.

Rethel, Lena (2010a) 'The New Financial Development Paradigm and Asian Bond Markets', *New Political Economy* 15(4), pp. 493–517.

Rethel, Lena (2010b) 'Financialisation and the Malaysian Political Economy', *Globalizations* 7(4), pp. 489–506.

Rethel, Lena (2011) 'Whose Legitimacy? Islamic Finance and the Global Financial Order', *Review of International Political Economy* 18(1), February, pp. 75–98.

Rethel, Lena (2012) 'Each Time Is Different! The Shifting Boundaries of Emerging Market Debt', *Global Society* 26(1), pp. 123–43.

Rochet, Jean-Charles (2010) 'The Future of Banking Regulation', in Mathias Dewatripont, Jean-Charles Rochet and Jean Tirole (eds), *Balancing the Banks*, Princeton NJ and Oxford: Princeton University Press, pp. 78–106.

Rodrik, Dani (2009) 'A Plan B for Global Finance', *The Economist*, 12 March.

Rosas, Guillermo (2009) *Curbing Bailouts*, Ann Arbor: University of Michigan Press.

Rosenbluth, Frances, and Ross Schaap (2003) 'The Domestic Politics of Banking Regulation', *International Organization* 57(2), pp. 307–36.

Roubini, Nouriel (2008) 'Next: The Mother of All Bank Runs', *Forbes*, 2 October, www.forbes.com/2008/10/01/goldman-morgan-run-oped-cx_nr_1002roubini. html; accessed 16 July 2011.

Rubin, Robert, and Jacob Weisberg (2003) *In an Uncertain World*, New York: Random House.

Seabrooke, Leonard (2010) 'What Do I Get? The Everyday Politics of Expectations and the Subprime Crisis', *New Political Economy* 15(1), pp. 51–70.

Searle, John R. (1969) *Speech Acts: An Essay in the Philosophy of Language*, Cambridge: Cambridge University Press.

Searle, John R. (2005) 'What is an Institution?' *Journal of Institutional Economics* 1(1), pp. 1–22.

Shiller, Robert J. (2011) 'Democratizing and Humanizing Finance', in Randall S. Kroszner and Robert J. Shiller (eds), *Reforming U.S. Financial Markets: Reflections Before and Beyond Dodd–Frank*, Cambridge MA: MIT Press.

Sinclair, Timothy J. (2005) *The New Masters of Capital: American Bond Rating Agencies and the Politics of Creditworthiness*, Ithaca NY: Cornell University Press.

Sinclair, Timothy J. (2009) 'The Queen and the Perfect Bicycle', *Inside Story*, 12 August 12, http://inside.org.au/the-queen-and-the-perfect-bicycle.

Sinclair, Timothy J. (2010a) 'Credit Rating Agencies and the Global Financial Crisis', *Economic Sociology: The European Electronic Newsletter*, 12(1), pp. 4–9, http://econsoc.mpifg.de.

Sinclair, Timothy J. (2010b) 'Round up the Usual Suspects: Blame and the Subprime Crisis', *New Political Economy* 15(1), pp. 91–107.

Sinclair, Timothy J. (2011) 'Stay on Target! Implications of the Global Financial Crisis for Asian Capital Markets', *Contemporary Politics* 17(2), pp. 119–31.

Sinclair, Timothy J. (2012) *Global Governance*. Cambridge: Polity Press.

Singh, Supriya (1984) *Bank Negara Malaysia: The First 25 Years*, Kuala Lumpur: Bank Negara Malaysia.

Skully, Michael T. (1984) (ed.) *Financial Institutions and Markets in Southeast Asia*, New York: St Martin's Press.

Stein, Benjamin J. (1992) *A License to Steal: The Untold Story of Michael Milken and the Conspiracy to Bilk the Nation*, New York: Simon & Schuster.

Suchan, Stefan W. (2004) 'Post-Enron: U.S. and German Corporate Governance', Cornell Law School LL.M. Papers Series 4, Cornell Law School, http://lsr. nellco.org/cornell/lps/papers/4; accessed 30 April 2005.

Sylla, Richard, Robert E. Wright and David J. Cowen (2009) 'Alexander Hamilton, Central Banker: Crisis Management during the U.S. Financial Panic of 1792', *Business History Review* 83(1), pp. 61–86.

Taleb, Nassim Nicholas (2010) *The Black Swan: The Impact of the Highly Improbable*, rev. edn, London: Penguin.

Tamaki, Norio (1995) *Japanese Banking: A History, 1859–1959*, Cambridge: Cambridge University Press.

Taylor, Michael, and Sara Singleton (1993) 'The Communal Resource: Trans-actions Costs and the Solution of Collective Action Problems', *Politics and Society* 21, pp. 195–214.

Thirkell-White, Ben (2009) 'Dealing with the Banks: Populism and the Public Interest in the Global Financial Crisis', *International Affairs* 85(4), pp. 689–711.

Thompson, Grahame (2010) '"Financial Globalisation" and the "Crisis": A Criti-cal Assessment and "What is to be Done"?', *New Political Economy* 15(1), pp. 127–45.

Thompson, John (2009) 'Current and Structural Developments in the Financial Systems of OECD Enhanced Engagement Countries', *Financial Market Trends* 2009(2), pp. 209–64.

Tilly, Charles (1992) *Coercion, Capital and European States, AD 990–1992*, Oxford: Blackwell.

Timewell, Stephen (2010) 'New World Order', *The Banker*, 6 July, www.thebanker. com/Banker-Data/Banker-Rankings/New-World-Order; accessed 14 January 2011.

Tirole, Jean (2010) 'Lessons from the Crisis', in Mathias Dewatripont, Jean-Charles Rochet and Jean Tirole (eds), *Balancing the Banks*, Princeton NJ and Oxford: Princeton University Press, pp. 10–77.

Toffler, Alvin (1990) *Powershift: Knowledge, Wealth, and Violence at the Edge of the 21st Century*, New York: Bantam.

Treasury Select Committee (2008) *The Run on the Rock*, Fifth Report of Session 2007–8, www.publications.parliament.uk/pa/cm200708/cmselect/cmtreasy/ 56/56i.pdf; accessed 16 July 2011.

Treasury Select Committee (2009) *Banking Crisis: Reforming Corporate Govern-ance and Pay in the City*, Ninth Report of Session 2008–9, www.publications. parliament.uk/pa/cm200809/cmselect/cmtreasy/519/519.pdf; accessed 16 July 2011.

Triffin, Robert (1961) *Gold and the Dollar Crisis: The Future of Convertibility*, rev. edn, New Haven CT and London: Yale University Press.

Tsingou, Eleni (2007) 'The Role of Policy Communities in Global Financial Gov-ernance: A Critical Examination of the Group of Thirty', in Torsten Strulik and Helmut Willke (eds), *Towards a Cognitive Mode in Global Finance*, Chicago: University of Chicago Press, 2007, pp. 213–37.

Uchitelle, Louis (2010) 'Glass–Steagall vs the Volcker Rule', *New York Times*, 22 January 2010.

Vanberg, Viktor J. (2011) 'The Freiburg School: Walter Eucken and Ordoliberalism', *Freiburg Discussion Papers on Constitutional Economics*, Freiburg: Albert-Lud-wigs University.

Vogel, Steven K. (1996) *Freer Markets, More Rules: Regulatory Reform in Advanced Industrial Countries*, Ithaca NY and London: Cornell University Press.

Volcker, Paul (2010) Interview by Chrystia Freeland for the *Financial Times*, 12 February, www.ft.com/cms/s/0/780d9d64-175d-11df-87f6-00144feab49a.html; accessed 22 June 2011.

Walter, Andrew (2008) *Governing Finance: East Asia's Adoption of International Standards*, Ithaca NY: Cornell University Press.

Wessel, David (2009) *In Fed We Trust: Ben Bernanke's War on the Great Panic*, New York: Crown Business.

White, Eugene Nelson (1982) 'The Political Economy of Banking Regulation, 1864–1933', *Journal of Economic History* 42(1), pp. 33–40.

White House (2010) Remarks by the President on Financial Reform, 21 January, www.whitehouse.gov/the-press-office/remarks-president-financial-reform; accessed: 22 June 2011.

Williamson, Oliver E. (1985) *The Economic Institutions of Capitalism*, New York: Simon & Schuster.

Wintour, Patrick (2011) 'Nick Clegg Calls for Public to Get Shares in Bailed-out Banks', www.guardian.co.uk, 23 June.

Yadav, Vikash (2008) *Risk in International Finance*, London: Routledge.

Yago, Glenn (1991) *Junk Bonds: How High Yield Securities Restructured Corporate America*, New York: Oxford University Press.

Zysman, John (1983) *Governments, Markets and Growth: Financial Systems and the Politics of Industrial Change*, Ithaca NY and London: Cornell University Press.

INDEX

ABOUT ZED BOOKS

Zed Books is a critical and dynamic publisher, committed to increasing awareness of important international issues and to promoting diversity, alternative voices and progressive social change. We publish on politics, development, gender, the environment and economics for a global audience of students, academics, activist and general readers. Run as a co-operative, we aim to operate in an ethical and environmentally sustainable way.

Find out more at
www.zedbooks.co.uk

For up-to-date news, articles, reviews
and events information visit
http://zed-books.blogspot.com

To subscribe to the monthly Zed Books e-newsletter
send an email headed 'subscribe' to marketing@zedbooks.net

We can also be found on Facebook, ZNet,
Twitter and Library Thing.